P9-DDY-113

THE
Caregiving
Season

FINDING GRACE TO HONOR YOUR AGING PARENTS

Jane Daly

Tyndale House Publishers, Inc.
Carol Stream, Illinois

Library of Congress Cataloging-in-Publication Data

Names: Daly, Jane S., author.
Title: The caregiving season : finding grace to honor your aging parents /Jane S. Daly.
Description: First Edition. | Carol Stream, Illinois : Tyndale House Publishers, 2016. | "A Focus on the Family book." | Includes bibliographical references and index.
Identifiers: LCCN 2016016393 | ISBN 9781589978690 (alk. paper)
Subjects: LCSH: Caregivers—Religious life. | Adult children of aging parents—Religious life. | Aging parents—Care—Religious aspects—Christianity. | Caring—Religious aspects—Christianity. | Aging—Religious aspects—Christianity.
Classification: LCC BV4910.9 .D35 2016 | DDC 248.8/4—dc23 LC record available at https://lccn.loc.gov/2016016393

Jane Daly has done all of us baby boomers with aging parents a huge favor. She has allowed us into her life as she and her husband, Mike, faced the challenges of "being there" during the declining years of her parents' lives. Full of empathy and practical advice, this book is a must for readers who are living through the caregiving season of life.

NIC ~~248.84 DAL~~

Auth~~~

The Care~~~ oped for: It encourag~~~ nable advice and time~~~ ught-through experiences, and careful considerations of the Scriptures and a variety of other valuable resources make this book the best I have seen on how to care for our loved ones—specifically the elderly among us. It has become my go-to book when counseling those who are in "the caregiving season."

DR. MARTY TRAMMELL
Humanities chair, Corban University; worship and family pastor, Valley Baptist of Perrydale; and coauthor of *Redeeming Relationships*, *Spiritual Fitness: A Guide to Biblical Maturity*, and *Communication Matters*

For all of us who have aging parents this book provides much-needed insight into how we can be our best for them in this challenging stage of life. Jane's stories ring true in every chapter. How do you explain to your father that it's not safe for him to drive anymore? Will your mother understand when you need to bring in additional care for her so that you can go out of state for your son's college graduation? The answers are here in this tenderly crafted book.

ROBIN JONES GUNN
Best-selling author of the Sisterchicks series and *Victim of Grace*

Experience is the best teacher . . . especially other people's experiences! I've had the wonderful privilege of getting to know Jane and Mike Daly and then reading this book cover to cover in a single evening. Both provide generous doses of good humor and practical wisdom. I so appreciate learning from their realistic, grounded, and ultimately hope-filled experiences. You will too!

DAVID SANFORD
General editor, *Handbook on Thriving as an Adoptive Family*

The Caregiving Season is an excellent story that will be understood by families who, at some time in their lives, will accept the responsibility of eldercare. For those who are just entering into it, this book will give them an idea of how to prepare. For those in the midst of their caregiving season, it will be reassurance for decisions they must make. And for those who finally say their last good-bye to a loved one, the life lessons gained from Daly's mentoring spirit will confirm to them that their extra measure of care was worth it.

J. STEVEN HUNT
Author of *Love and Deception: One Family's Encounter with Dementia*

This is a very practical and useful tool. After providing eighteen-plus years of pastoral care, I can say that I will use and give this book to others. Well done!

DAN WADE
Pastor of Congregational Care, River City Christian Church, Sacramento, CA

In this excellent read about caregiving for aging and dependent parents, Jane describes the bittersweet moments, heartfelt dialogues, and tearful moments she's had with her own parents. A beautifully written book that is filled with numerous anecdotes that will have you laughing or in tears and ultimately growing more compassion for the aged and oneself.

CHARLENE HONG
Licensed marriage and family therapist

This book is dedicated to all the men
and women of "the Greatest Generation."
Thank you for your strength and endurance during
difficult times. Your example is not forgotten.

CONTENTS

FOREWORD

They say growing old isn't for sissies. Caring for elderly parents might be in that same "not-for-sissies" category.

Watching your mom grow dependent or realizing your dad's mind isn't what it used to be is difficult on so many levels, and the added responsibility of caregiving creates a unique kind of stress. If you're caring for your parents, chances are you've added several time-consuming tasks to your schedule. And those tasks seem to be tied to a complex set of emotions.

As you drive your mother to the doctor, handle your father's finances, and shop for their groceries, you might be mourning the life they—and you—used to have. Then again, you might be angry with your folks, your siblings, or even God. Maybe you feel guilty that you live far away and are questioning every decision you must now make for your parents. Or you simply may be depressed and overwhelmed by finding yourself in a new, unexpected role. Plenty of caregivers are!

If you have this book in your hands, you are probably well aware of this stress. Yet you desire to honor your parents, even when it's difficult.

My brother Mike and his wife, Jane, understand. They've wrestled with a long list of emotions and difficult situations as they've spent years caring for Jane's mother and father. Early on, Jane decided that she wanted her caregiving to be characterized by grace, not resentment, bitterness, or impatience.

If you feel the same way, then this is the book for you. Whether you're just entering into the caregiving season or you're in the thick of it and feeling weary, this book can help you gain (or regain) a godly perspective.

I think that like me, you'll appreciate Jane's total honesty about her emotions and struggles. She isn't the perfect caregiver, and she's willing to admit that here. By the way, I hope you know that there's no such thing as a perfect caregiver. Instead there are simply people like Jane and Mike, who commit themselves to honoring their parents as God commands us to do in Exodus 20:12.

But how do you honor a parent who accuses you of stealing, upsets your household, or expects more than you can give? Jane not only addresses these challenges, she encourages caregivers to bring everything before the Lord, recognizing that His grace-filled love, unending strength, and promise of provision are vital to this mission.

In *The Caregiving Season*, Jane humbly shares what she learned as she was blindsided by her father's declining health. She reveals how she needed to examine certain attitudes and hand them over to Jesus. She invites you to cry, laugh, mourn, and seek the Lord with her as you both make your way through changing familial landscapes. As Jane did, you may also come to see this season as an opportunity to become more Christlike and dependent on

God. After all, it's only by seeking His grace that you can, in turn, offer it—over and over again—to your loved ones.

Over the years, I've seen how Jane and Mike have committed themselves wholeheartedly to this caregiving season. They have faithfully acted in love, giving their time, emotional support, and resources to honor Jane's folks in a tender, sacrificial way. Day after day, week after week, month after month, and year after year, this couple has paid the bills, made the meals, provided loving reassurance, sat at the doctor's office, and hauled the walker and wheelchair to and fro.

All this is to say that Jane has been where you might be now. So come sit with a friend who understands. I'm confident that you'll come away with a renewed sense of purpose, a refreshed spirit, and tools that will help you honor your aging parents with grace.

Jim Daly
President, Focus on the Family

INTRODUCTION

If you're a baby boomer as I am, chances are you're finding yourself in a new phase of life and it's a bit of a shock. As a boomer, you've been leading a busy life, perhaps holding down a career as you enjoy your teenagers' last years in high school. Or maybe you've been reveling in your empty nest as you travel, visit grandchildren, and pursue personal interests that were put aside during the child-raising years. Then Mom fell, or Dad developed dementia, and everything changed. You never expected to be tethered to your parents. Neither did I.

Yet according to a recent CNN report, caregiving for loved ones is the new normal for boomers.[1] That's not surprising, considering that the number of older Americans increased by 18 percent between 2000 and 2011, compared with an increase of 9.4 percent for those under 65. And the older population is increasingly older: In 2011, the 65–74 age group was almost ten times larger than in 1900; the 75–84 group was sixteen times larger, and the 85-plus group was forty times larger.[2]

Even though I knew the Greatest Generation (those who came of age during the Great Depression and fought in World War II) was living longer, this reality didn't hit home until I saw my mom's and dad's health declining. Would I have to begin making choices for them? Choices they weren't able to make for themselves? Yet the caregiving season begins whether or not we're ready for it.

As Christians, we don't take lightly God's command in Exodus 20:12, "Honor your father and your mother, so that you may live long in the land the LORD your God is giving you."

Again in Matthew 15:4, Jesus said, "For God said, 'Honor your father and mother' and 'Anyone who curses his father or mother must be put to death.'"

If I lived in Old Testament times, I could expect to be dragged into the street and stoned if I didn't fulfill the law. These days, no one holds us accountable, and it's human nature to read these commands and simply pass over them, maybe giving a nod to their timeless truth.

Yes, I think, *I should honor my father and mother . . . until they get on my last nerve!*

Jesus goes on to say in the same passage that if a person isn't willing to help his parents with physical needs, he is a hypocrite.

Lord, am I a hypocrite? I do want to do right and take care of my parents. But won't it require too much of my time? And money? And take away my freedom?

Interestingly, other cultures don't seem to struggle with this as much as natural-born Americans do. In many Asian and Hispanic households, it's common to find two or three generations living under one roof. It's expected that the younger ones will care for their elders. Independent Americans don't as readily consider others when making decisions about where to live, or whether to take a job that would require moving away from family.

I've had many conversations with my husband, Mike, about moving closer to his family, rather than staying close to mine. We've always circled back to the reality of my parents' needs. We couldn't go anywhere else. Who would take care of Mom and Dad? Even now at times I want to jump in the car and go, leaving behind the caregiving responsibility. It's a perpetual tug-of-war between God's will and mine. You may be struggling with the same emotions and questions.

As our parents' health declines and our care for them increases, we may find ourselves battling with guilt, negotiating new boundaries, and dealing with exhaustion. Often we're the brunt of our parents' anger and frustration over their dependence on others. And even if we rarely doubt ourselves when making decisions for our own children, making decisions while caring for elderly parents is especially difficult.

Nevertheless, I've discovered through my caregiving season that we *can* find help from the Source of Peace throughout this emotionally wrenching experience. We can turn from dependence upon our own strength, and even from dependence upon our parents, to dependence upon Christ. Isn't that we hope for in this and every circumstance?

The more I thought about this season in which I found myself, the more I became convinced this was the greatest opportunity yet for God to transform me into the image of His Son (2 Corinthians 3:18). Learning to be caregivers for our mothers and fathers *can* be a journey of spiritual growth if we allow it. As I fought against giving up my empty-nest lifestyle and accepting my altered relationship with my parents, God taught me how to continue through this season with grace.

I've also learned that just as changing leaves herald the fall and flying snow signifies winter, there are certain signposts of the caregiving season. First come feelings of denial and loss. It's not always easy to accept the reality of your parents' mortality and acknowledge their losses—and ours. As caregivers, we may lose some independence for a season. Yet if we compare those losses with the changes our parents are facing and take our frustrations to the Lord, we have the opportunity to grow in grace while discovering the beauty of interdependence.

After we move beyond denial, we may find ourselves trying to make bargains as we work through the adjusted schedules and emotional pitfalls that caregiving can bring. We might try to strike bargains with ourselves, our parents, our siblings, and even God. Yet will we seek God's grace when we most desperately need it and when we most desperately need to offer it to our parents and ourselves?

If we're able to do so, we can learn to accept our new roles, transform more deeply into the likeness of Christ, and help our parents make their final decisions before they exit this world.

This season is difficult, yet rewarding. You will find yourself stretched beyond measure, yet blessed in many surprising ways. Come along with me on a journey through the caregiving season. May my experiences and those of others encourage you as you move into this new stage of life with your aging loved one.

PART I

ACKNOWLEDGING LOSS

1

SEEING THE SIGNS

When I was a child, I talked like a child, I thought
like a child, I reasoned like a child. When I
became a man, I put childish ways behind me.

1 CORINTHIANS 13:11

O ur world finally seemed perfect. After a long season as
parents of two amazing, happy kids, we no longer had the
responsibilities that came with having them at home. I'd started a
new job with a huge pay increase. We traveled, ate out, and spent
a lot of time with friends.

Life was good. Until things changed. One day several years
ago, I noticed some damage to my parents' garage door.

"Did you see my folks' garage?" I asked my husband, Mike.

"No, why?"

Mike and I live in the same townhome complex as my parents.
They live at one end of the row, and we live at the other.

"One side of the door is splintered," I explained.

Mike walked down to look. He reported that it looked like
someone had clipped the side of the garage.

A few days later at dinner, Mike asked my dad about the damage. Dad harrumphed a few times. Mom told us Dad's foot slipped off the brake when he pulled in.

"I wouldn't have expected it to gouge the side like that," Mike pressed.

After some roundabout explanation, Mom said that perhaps Dad wasn't exactly pointed straight when pulling into the garage. Mike and I exchanged a look, but we laughed it off, ignoring the first warnings of my father's diminishing capacity. Small dings and bumps on the car could happen to anyone. I'd been known to back into parking lot pillars. As simple as that, we slipped into the river of denial.

Later, I learned that many senior drivers don't realize their eyesight, hearing, and reflexes aren't as sharp as they used to be. They may be taking medication that impairs judgment, memory, or coordination, or they may suffer from arthritis or Alzheimer's disease. They may not realize it when they blow past a stop sign, forget to signal a turn, or confuse the gas pedal with the brake.[1]

The Centers for Disease Control and Prevention cites some scary statistics: more than 500 older drivers are injured daily in car accidents, with an average of fifteen killed *every day*.

> Per mile, fatalities increase at age seventy and notably after age eighty-five, "largely due to increased susceptibility to injury and medical complications among older drivers."
> Declines in vision, cognitive function, and physical abilities affect many older adults as well.
> "Across all age groups, males [have] substantially higher death rates than females."[2]

KING OF THE ROAD

My dad grew up on a farm in rural Pennsylvania in the early 1930s and learned to drive a tractor when he was twelve. He and his younger brother worked hard alongside their father, an immigrant from Germany, and driving young was a given.

When the United States entered World War II, my dad enlisted and my parents were stationed in Arizona. Whenever my father had a three-day pass, my folks would drive from Arizona to Los Angeles to visit my grandparents. From that time until he died, road trips were my dad's favorite pastime. After the military, his job as a salesman for General Electric gave him the opportunity to be on the road three or four days a week during my childhood. He'd think nothing of loading us kids into the station wagon and driving somewhere on the weekend. Perhaps that's why I love riding in the car.

I was twenty when my parents decided to visit Germany and buy a car there. Their plan was to pick it up in Stuttgart, then drive it around Europe for a month before having it shipped back to the States. They invited my grandma, Nini, to go along, and she invited me. Nini didn't want to be a fifth wheel, as she called it. In Europe, Dad confidently took control, driving us from Germany to Austria, Switzerland, France, Italy, and Spain. There was no question about who the driver would be.

When my parents were sixty years old, they built their third motel an hour and a half from their home. To give the manager a day off, they made the drive to that motel every week for twenty years. After they retired, Dad and Mom enjoyed frequent day trips to some of the beautiful places in northern California. When the four of us would take a day trip, my dad always drove.

It was his thing. In his generation, men drove; women were the passengers. I can't remember ever seeing my mom take turns driving on a long trip.

Dad became the family taxi driver when my mother's macular degeneration worsened to the point where she was legally blind. They climbed into the car almost every day to run errands. I'd see their red Jeep pass by my living room window and I'd think, "Where are they going this time?"

I was proud my folks were independent. Dad and Mom continued to take their trips to the mountains, they played bridge every week with a group of other retired folks, and they met regularly with friends for dinner and bridge. It seemed like they were always on the go.

After reading a newspaper article about a 101-year-old woman who backed up and plowed into eleven elementary school children, I was grateful my dad could still get around safely without help. Even into his eighties, Dad was robust. He was quick-witted and laughed easily. His interests were varied. He read voraciously, loved using the computer, and knew enough about electricity to be dangerous. His greatest joy was to come home from a morning of garage sale shopping with a bargain. I'd often have lunch or coffee with him, and he always asked about my work. "You're the Queen Bee there," he'd tell me.

DETOUR AHEAD

Several months after the garage door incident, we were having dinner with my parents when my mom asked, "Do you know how to get hold of Henry? We need him to do some work." Henry is the maintenance man for our townhome complex.

"What are you having done?" Mike asked as he gave Mom the phone number.

My parents exchanged a look. "Dad crashed into the side of the garage."

"Again?" I exclaimed.

> No matter what the relationship was between the parent and child—whatever it was—[caring for your parents] is going to be extremely challenging because *it is not logical.* There's no way to deal with it rationally or directly. You don't reason it out. What I've said to so many people is: we always must lead with our love.
>
> **DR. STEPHEN HOAG**
> *A Son's Handbook: Bringing Up Mom*
> *with Alzheimer's/Dementia*

Mom told us that Dad couldn't get his foot from the gas pedal to the brake pedal in time to stop.

We knew Dad had been having some issues with weakness and pain in his legs, but I didn't realize it had become that bad. Fear swept over me, as did a premonition that life was about to change. Was there more to this than just a small fender bender? Was my eighty-five-year-old dad losing his mind? Would he turn into someone I didn't recognize?

I'd seen this happen to other people as they aged. When my grandmother suffered a series of small strokes, her short-term memory and some of her long-term memory disappeared. Our conversations went like this:

"What's new in your world?" Nini would ask.

I'd tell her about my job, the kids, and Mike. When I was finished, she'd sip her coffee, looking off into the distance.

After a few seconds of silence, she'd turn to face me again and ask, "So what's new in your world?"

Eventually she forgot who I was.

Would Dad become forgetful too? I couldn't seem to face Dad's diminishing capacity. In my mind, step one was to quit driving, step two would be moving directly to an assisted-living facility, and step three was death.

In the next few days and weeks, Mike and I talked endlessly about what we should do. Was it time to talk with Dad about giving up his driver's license? What would that mean for us? Mike worked thirty minutes away from home. I was still in the early months of my new job. Who would take Mom and Dad to the doctor, the pharmacy, the grocery store? My biggest fear was this: telling my dad that I was taking away his driver's license—his ticket to independence and freedom.

Millions of older drivers have never had so much as a speeding ticket in years of driving. Many self-regulate themselves by driving less often and avoiding frightening high-speed highways. But they can still be a menace on neighborhood streets. A *Consumer Reports* article I read states, "People eighty and older are involved in 5.5 times as many fatal crashes per mile driven as middle-aged drivers."[3] I was terrified Dad wouldn't be able to stop at a crosswalk filled with children.

I could see Dad being responsible for some gruesome traffic

accident with dead bodies strewn on the street. Or he'd hit a light pole and be killed. I remembered one time when Mom told me Dad had drifted into oncoming traffic and she had to yell at him. He jerked back into the correct lane, but Mom was frightened. We had to do something. But if Dad couldn't drive Mom around, who would? Did I have to give up my life to become a taxi service for my folks?

My prayers were requests for strength to find the words to say to Dad and wisdom in saying them. I prayed for peace, for relief from my fears, and for God to keep me from being selfish. I was worried that more would be required of me than I was willing to give.

My dad always called me "Chickie" and "Queen Bee." His encouragement through the years gave me the will to succeed at whatever I put my mind to. He repeatedly told me, "You can do anything you want." Whether he was dispensing advice ("When it stops being fun, quit") or asking his usual question ("Do you need any walking-around money?"), his love for me was evident.

How could I ask my dad to stop doing the one thing he loved doing above all else? I wanted my oldest brother to step up and call a family meeting so I didn't have to lose my place as the adored baby of the family. Giving up this role would be the first of the losses I would face.

One of my friends reported her dad to the Department of Motor Vehicles because she was afraid for his safety. When it came time to renew his license, he was informed it was cancelled. To my friend's chagrin, her father continued to drive. He totaled his car, bought another, and had a fender bender in that one.

She tried taking the keys away. Her dad had a spare set. She took those, too. He walked across the street to his neighbors' house and borrowed their car! He finally gave up driving, but the process involved a lot of "kicking and screaming"—on both their parts.

Would Mike and I have to go through the same thing to get my dad to stop driving?

BE ANXIOUS FOR NOTHING

Over the following weeks, there would be many such moments of questioning and preparing myself for the changes to come. As I suspected, this was only the start of losses for Dad . . . and for me. I felt the beginning of the end of my father's vibrant life. I knew my life would change, and I was anxious. My dad was anxious too, though he didn't show it outwardly. He hated to depend on anyone, especially his Chickie. As my distress over my dad's loss of function mounted, I was brought back to 1 Peter 5:7: "Cast all your anxiety on him, because he cares for you."

Since that time, I've learned that it's vital to have discussions with our elderly loved ones about how they view their final years. Consider their vision of the future and see if it matches reality. It's also important to talk about how much care you can reasonably provide. Talk about the "what-ifs." What if they need in-home care? What if one or both parents need to move into an assisted-living facility? What if you're not available to help? As you begin to consider the questions, be ready to present your parents with various options to help alleviate any fears about the future.

Most states and counties offer services for seniors. The website SeniorAdvisor.com compares housing options for most states and

Canada. The cost of public transportation is discounted for the elderly, and many counties offer door-to-door service for visually impaired or disabled seniors. Taxis and private transportation companies like Uber and Lyft are also an alternative to driving. Many grocery stores deliver. Once you've seen the warning signs, it's time to consider what services your parents may need to continue living independently.

Grace Growers

1. Has your elderly loved one shown signs of loss of function? Consider how you can prayerfully begin a discussion about the changes you and they can expect as the months and years progress.

2. It's difficult to watch your parents growing older. Consider your relationship as their child, and ask yourself how that role may change. How will you show them grace as they begin to expect more from you? Read 1 Corinthians 13:11. Consider ways in which you still think or act like a child. Ask God to show you how you can, with grace, begin to come alongside your parents in this season of loss.

3. Meditate on 1 Peter 5:7. Make a conscious effort to take your anxiety to Jesus, and allow Him to carry it. Picture Him walking beside you, holding your hand as you journey into the caregiving season.

2
DAD, CAN I HAVE THE CAR KEYS?

What I'd really like, Dad, is to borrow the car keys.
See you later, can I have them please?

HARRY CHAPIN, "CAT'S IN THE CRADLE"

Who doesn't remember saying those words? When we were teenagers, the keys to the family car represented freedom from parental oversight. It was a chance for us to spread our wings and experience the joy of conquering another milestone in the march toward adulthood. Little did we realize then that we might one day *dread* asking our parents for their car keys.

When my mother's eyesight began to fail in her early eighties, her life changed dramatically. She had four passions: crossword puzzles, reading, bridge, and baking. I purchased books of giant-sized puzzles. I scoured the library for large-print books. I took her to the Society for the Blind to buy beaded measuring cups and spoons, digital clocks that could easily be seen, and a wristwatch that spoke the time. Mom handed over her driver's license, but not without a fight.

"I can still see far away," she insisted.

"What if a little kid runs out in front of the car?" I asked.

She didn't have an answer. She knew logically she shouldn't drive, but after more than sixty years of jumping in the car and going whenever and wherever she wanted, it stung to admit defeat. She knew it was the first of many small steps toward dependence upon others.

Her inability to see caused depression to settle in, and soon Mom stopped cooking altogether. My folks started driving to fast-food restaurants almost every night. They were like two out-of-control teenagers, constantly eating hamburgers, fish and chips, tacos, and pizza. Their freezer was always stocked with ice cream, and sweet pastries became a breakfast staple.

At least my dad's eyes were still good at that point, and he was able to drive Mom anywhere. I think they made up places to go, just to get out of the house.

"I need trash bags from Kmart, trail mix from Target, groceries from WinCo, and my prescription from CVS," my mother would say.

I'd ask why she couldn't buy everything from WinCo, but she'd insist that Kmart was the only place that had the trash bags she liked. It was the same story for each item. Some days my folks bragged about the number of stops they'd made in a day.

But after my dad's second heart attack, my parents' lives began to slow down. They still took regular trips to Reno or Tahoe, but spent the night instead of making the round trip in one day. Occasionally they'd take the bus or the train, but it wasn't the same for Dad. He had to be behind the wheel. The freeway between Sacramento and Reno was one he had traveled for twelve years as a salesman. He knew every curve of the road, every gas station, and every rest stop. He could have driven it with his eyes closed.

THE END OF THE ROAD

Then one day Dad noticed a tingling in his legs. I'd see him on the couch, rubbing his legs, first the left, then the right, wincing as he did. I didn't like it. I realized I still saw him from a child's eyes. Surely he wasn't getting "elderly." He'd always been there in the background of my life, a strong constant, my hero and benign sage. With shame I had to admit that some part of me still believed he would live forever, and I'd always be his "Chickie."

After rounds of doctor's appointments, Dad was diagnosed with neuropathy (nerve damage), a common issue in the aged. There was no medical solution, nothing to help stop its progression. The tingling soon turned into intense pain and weakness. He began to have trouble getting around. But he stubbornly kept driving.

When Dad ran into the garage the second time, my stomach sank.

"What should we do?" I asked Mike.

The one thing that unites all human beings, regardless of age, gender, religion, economic status, or ethnic background, is that, deep down inside, we all believe that we are above-average drivers.

DAVE BARRY
Humorist

"We just have to tell him he can't drive."

"Right. Like that'll be easy." My mind played and replayed potential conversations.

Dad, you can't drive anymore. Nope. Too direct.

Dad, we've noticed your driving has become a little erratic. Better.

Mom is worried about your driving. That's it—make Mom the bad guy.

Mike assured me everything would be fine. "Just pray about it," he advised.

Sure, easy enough to say. I'd use my will to turn the situation over to the Lord, and then grab it back. This tug-of-war continued, despite my best efforts. A distant memory verse kept coming to the surface. The context wasn't important to me at the time, but the meaning was clear. "With man this is impossible, but with God all things are possible" (Matthew 19:26). I knew God's strength is made perfect in my weakness. So I claimed these truths as my own. It helped—when I remembered.

The next step was explaining to Mom that if Dad couldn't move his foot fast enough from gas pedal to brake pedal, there could be serious consequences. I quoted the article about the eighty-year-old man who drove his car into a McDonald's, killing some kids. She relented and agreed to support Mike and me when we talked to Dad. But she wouldn't start the conversation. I had to be the enforcer, the deliverer of bad news.

I never pictured my parents' decline. I was still the ten-year-old child, wanting my parents' approval.

I remembered showing off in our swimming pool.

Daddy, watch me! I can swim two and a half laps underwater without taking a breath!

At twelve, *Daddy, I read this 600-page book!*

At twenty-one, *Dad, I want to introduce you to the man I'm going to marry.*

I can still hear his laugh, see his smile.

That's great, Chickie.

How could I possibly take away Dad's car keys? He was the one who taught me to drive. The first time I climbed behind the wheel, Dad instructed me to back slowly out of the driveway into the street. I didn't think the car was going fast enough, so I pressed my foot on the accelerator and gunned it. We shot across the street, straight into the neighbor's station wagon, parked in front of their house.

We jumped out of the car to examine the damage. Thankfully, the neighbor was more gracious than I deserved. He meandered down his driveway, looked at the dent in the door, and commented, "Well, I guess it'll match the dent in the other side."

Dad made me get behind the wheel and try again, after apologizing profusely to the neighbor. Eventually, I became comfortable behind the wheel. Dad's patience and longsuffering calmed me when I was ready to freak out in heavy traffic. He gently prodded me to take the car on the freeway, instructing me on the correct way to merge. He told me I'd know I had "arrived" when I stopped thinking about the details and began driving naturally. He was right.

THE TALK

Mike and I prayed before walking to my parents' place. My feet grew heavier with each step. I was carrying a ticking time bomb. I'd toss it into my parents' living room, and then be forced to remain while it exploded. I expected stinging questions like shards of shrapnel.

"How will we get around?"

"Who will take care of us?"

"Will we be stuck in the house forever?"

"If I can't drive, why would I want to live?"

Concerns of suicide among the elderly are valid. Even among those who've survived wars, economic depressions, recessions, friends' deaths, and financial failure, not being able to drive can seem worse. Like most Americans, elderly people place a high value on freedom and independence.

The *New York Times* reports that suicides among women decline after age sixty, but the rate among men keeps climbing. The *Times* article included these statistics: "Elderly white men have the highest rate: 29 per 100,000 overall, and more than 47 per 100,000 among those over age 85."[1] Because depression is the most common risk factor for suicide, I worried about my dad's mental health if he couldn't drive. The article also noted that "men are good at masking [depression], since [they've] been conditioned to believe it's not okay to express emotional pain."[2]

We arrived at my parents' house. My dad was delighted, as usual, that we'd come for a visit. My nerves jangled as Mom brewed a pot of coffee.

I'm a horrible daughter. I can't do this. I'm a traitor. Mike's calm resolve was the only thing keeping me from running out the door. Guilt weighed heavy on my shoulders.

"So what's new?" Dad asked.

Mike took a deep breath and started the conversation.

"Dad, did you see that news report a few weeks ago? The one

about the guy losing control of his car and killing some pedestrians?"

"Sure, that was bad."

"It turns out he was an older guy and couldn't move his foot from the gas to the brake."

The four of us agreed that tragedy shouldn't have happened.

"Remember how you had that incident with the side of the garage?" Mike continued. "We're all worried something like that might happen to you."

The grenade was launched. Tick, tick, tick.

I waited for the explosion.

It never came. Dad understood, and he agreed he didn't want to be a menace on the road.

I took a deep breath, thanking God for a miracle. I *wasn't* the worst daughter in the world, the person who had deprived my dad of his only life pleasure.

GOOD-BYE, FREEDOM

To compensate for my guilt, I said I'd be willing to drive my folks on their errands. I'd take my dad to the swap meet early Sunday mornings so he could hang out with his buddies. We'd bond over garage sales. My mom and I would do our shopping together at WinCo every Saturday. I felt so good. It was easy to try to make the best of the situation. I went home with the most hope I'd felt in weeks.

Reality set in as Mom and I set off for grocery shopping the next weekend. I saw my future as endless days of errands stacked up against me, and it felt like prison. Every weekend from now on would be gobbled up by my parents' ever-increasing needs.

I wasn't ready to exchange my role as adult child for one of caregiver. But most of all, I wasn't ready to give up my freedom. Things were changing. Truthfully, I was looking only at *my* loss, *my* time, and *my* freedom. I couldn't yet see my parents through the eyes of grace. God's Holy Spirit gently nudged me toward Him. I needed to pray.

As I prayed, I struggled with feelings of guilt and selfishness. But God spoke to me again, this time through Matthew 11:28: "Come to me, all you who are weary and burdened, and I will give you rest."

And then there's a beautiful hymn that helped me have an eternal perspective:

> *Turn your eyes upon Jesus,*
> *Look full in His wonderful face,*
> *And the things of earth will grow strangely dim*
> *In the light of His glory and grace.*[3]

When I turned my focus from myself and my perceived losses, I could more fully see His grace at work. He reminded me that this caregiving season was just that, a season.

A few weeks later, my sister-in-law told me about a driving service for shut-ins. For a nominal fee, my folks could hire a driver to take them on errands. I was elated. God answered my prayer in providing Violet. All Mom had to do was call a day ahead, and Violet would show up, ready to go. It was a match made in heaven.

A NEW IDENTITY

Depriving my dad of something he loved to do, ripping away his independence, his *manhood*, was painful. His identity was in his ability to be the provider. So often our self-worth is in outward circumstances. When Mike and I were missionaries in rural Montana, my identity was in my ability to be the perfect pastor's wife. Placing our identity in anything other than Jesus Christ is looking in the wrong direction.

When Dad lost part of his identity, he could have become angry and refused to stop driving. He could have pitched a fit, railed against the injustice of life, and lashed out at Mike and me. I was fortunate, and I believe our prayer and consideration of his loss helped prevent what could have become a strained relationship. Other friends told me that their struggle to wrestle the car keys from their mom or dad created an atmosphere of resentment.

As it worked out, despite the true loss of independence for Dad and for me, we learned something about freedom through that early experience with the reality of his aging. He learned that to give up driving wasn't as difficult as it could have been; I learned how to set aside my "time budget" and give more of my life to my parents. Becoming less selfish, a by-product of being the youngest child and the only girl, was a slow process. I remember something my mom said a long time ago: "We're a family, and that's what families do." We let go (loss), and we embrace what God has for us (gain).

Grace Growers

1. If you've broached the subject of driving, has it turned into a battle between you and your parents? How important is it for you to "win"? Philippians 2 tells us how to behave with one another. Read through the chapter to purify your motives and your heart as you continue to talk with your loved ones.

2. John 8:31–32 says, "To the Jews who had believed him, Jesus said, 'If you hold to my teaching, you are really my disciples. Then you will know the truth, and the truth will set you free.'" Consider your viewpoint regarding freedom. What does freedom mean from a Christian worldview? How can that truth help you as you adjust your schedule to care for your parents?

3

WHAT HAPPENED
TO MY DAD?

To appoint unto them that mourn in Zion, to give
unto them beauty for ashes, the oil of joy for
mourning, the garment of praise for the spirit
of heaviness; that they might be called trees of
righteousness, the planting of the LORD,
that he might be glorified.

ISAIAH 61:3 (KJV)

As we note the gradual day-to-day changes in those we love, the "big picture" transformations often elude us. Then in one moment, we may suddenly witness a decade or two pass before our eyes. Our children seem to be infants one day, and the next they're dressing up for prom, or walking down the aisle to meet their new spouse. The same thing happens with our parents, except in reverse. We forever see them as youthful, vibrant people, playing baseball with us in the backyard, challenging us to a game of Scrabble, or handing out wisdom around the dinner table. They're growing older, but in our mind's eye, they stay the same.

Because I lived near my parents, it was easy for me to remain in the role of child so I could frequently call on my mom and dad for help. I'd ask Mom to let the cat out while I was gone and Dad to meet the plumber or pick up my clothes from the dry cleaner's. In return I learned to accept, "Be careful coming home," "Make someone walk you to your car. It's dark out," and "Lock your doors and don't take candy from strangers." Okay, they didn't say that last one, but you get the picture.

There was a moment at my brother's house that jarred me from this status quo into chilling reality. We'd had the traditional Thanksgiving meal and were relaxing in the living room. Dad said he was cold, so my sister-in-law placed a soft throw across his lap.

Suddenly he burst out, "I'm not doing very well, in case anyone cares to ask." Conversation stopped, followed by awkward silence. I realized then that things were not okay and might never be okay again. I knew my parents were no longer young, no longer healthy. Now it hit me that someday not far off, and possibly sooner than later, they would *die.*

One of my earliest memories of my dad is when he took my brothers and me to Disneyland when I was about four. Because Dad worked for General Electric, we had passes to the VIP lounge. I'll never forget the look of delight on Dad's face as he watched my brothers and me stare with openmouthed awe at the wonder of Disneyland. His smile spread from one ear to the other. He stood tall and proud as we entered the GE lounge, feeling like a big shot as we were served food and sodas. He was my hero. He was thirty-seven years old and sitting on top of the world.

Now he was hunched over his walker, unable to walk more

than a few steps and feeling every moment of his eighty-eight years. His face wore the perpetual scowl of pain, his high spirits leeched out from living too long in a body that had betrayed him.

How had I missed his gradual decline? My world was knocked off balance as I tried to adjust to this old person who resembled my dad but didn't sound like him, talk like him, or act like him. In earlier years, his engaging personality and dry sense of humor had made him popular at social events. He had smiled often, laughed heartily, and was genuinely interested in people. My dad was generous and giving, with a hundred friends. This older guy was self-centered.

In all the times I remember asking, "Hi, Dad, how ya doing?" he'd always answer with a smile, "About average, I guess."

Now the answer exploded from him: "I hurt!"

PAIN AND PERSONALITY

Pain management in the elderly is a delicate balance. Concerns about side effects keep many aging parents from admitting pain. Others think chronic aches and pains are facts of life, so they don't bother to discuss their condition with a doctor. According to the National Institutes of Health, 50 percent of seniors living on their own and 75 to 85 percent of seniors in eldercare facilities experience chronic pain, yet most of it remains untreated.[1] Arthritis, neuropathy, central pain syndrome (associated with strokes), and repetitive strain injury (such as carpal tunnel) are common. Joints can become calcified, leading to loss of mobility. Sensation and balance decrease, and falls can happen.

My dad, stubborn German that he was, would take one or two muscle relaxants and then announce that they didn't work.

Telling him to give the medicine at least a week to bring relief was pointless.

"I'm not going to take something that doesn't work!" he'd shout. Then he would mutter all the way down the hall as he retreated to his bedroom. He didn't think I knew he kept a bottle of port wine between the bed and the nightstand. It may have marginally improved the constant ache in his legs, but it didn't help his surliness.

My friends Mark and Lisa are caregivers for Lisa's mom, Helen. Mark told me that Helen seems to like being disabled. She enjoys ordering others to do her bidding. Like a queen on a throne, she says whatever she likes at any particular moment. Apparently, she wasn't always such a demanding autocrat. Lisa remembers her mother staying up all night sewing a dress for Lisa to wear to the prom. Now she wonders, *When did that selfless woman morph into someone who barks orders and expects instant obedience? When did she become a neurotic, needy, self-centered drama queen?*

Several people I've talked with have said that their aging parents are more critical, grouchier, or more forgetful than ever. I remember one time my mother was being especially difficult. I called her on it. Her response?

"I'm old, so I can act any way I darn well choose."

My retort was just as pointed. "And I can choose not to be around you."

But when you carry the sole responsibility for your folks, it's not that easy. I couldn't just walk away from my parents.

For caregivers dealing with the effects of dementia or Alzheimer's disease, their parent's personality slowly changes as the disease progresses. Depression, medication, chronic pain, and aftereffects of a stroke or heart attack can also cause personality changes. That's another reason it's important to become a part of your parents' medical team. Ask for permission to go with them to appointments. Sometimes another set of ears can help, and sharing your loved ones' symptoms from your point of view may help the doctor make adjustments to medication.

LOVE ANYWAY

If making adjustments doesn't help a parent's attitude, we're still called to love that crotchety person. So how could I allow Christ's love to pour from me like a spring, when my flesh wanted to turn and run to the safety of home? I could show God's patience when I helped my dad to the car, and it took twenty minutes to move him from the wheelchair to the front seat. I could show God's love as I calmly folded up the chair, hoisted it into the back of the car, and drove to the doctor's office. It was the same process, in reverse, once we reached our destination.

Truth be told, my impatience showed itself more than once in my curt answers to Dad's questions.

"How you doing, Chickie?" he'd ask.

"Fine."

"Can you wrestle the wheelchair by yourself?"

"Yup," I'd answer, while I really thought, *Who else could help me? The only other person here is Jesus, and I desperately need His grace right now.*

John the Baptist said, "By myself I can do nothing" (John 5:30). Jesus also said, "Apart from me you can do nothing" (John 15:5). Without God's Holy Spirit, I'm unable to love. I need Jesus!

In order to grow in Christ, God presents us with inconvenient and unwanted interruptions to our plans—it could be a life-altering disability or dementia of an aging parent. Growth in Christ means learning how to deal morally and compassionately with these interruptions.

JONI EARECKSON TADA
Author

The Bible says, "Do not merely look out for your own personal interests, but also for the interests of others" (Philippians 2:4, NASB). I'm called to care for others, beginning with my own family. Scripture tells us that a man who doesn't care for his father or mother is worse than an infidel (see 1 Timothy 5:8). The word *infidel* is used in the King James Version, but the same word is translated as *unbeliever* in other translations. The comparison used in 1 Timothy sounds harsh. It's something I don't want to be accused of.

Life isn't fair. Showing God's grace through service can be inconvenient. As caregivers, we're often called upon to do things we're not comfortable doing. It can be a hassle stashing a cumbersome wheelchair in the trunk of your car. It's tiresome helping elderly parents in and out of a vehicle and being the interpreter between health care professionals and your loved one. One trip to the doctor can be exhausting. You might be annoyed, but take a step back and consider how your parents must feel as they face diminished capacities. When people first start "slipping," they are aware of the loss, and they are often terrified, scared, and saddened.

The hardest thing about caring for a loved one whose personality changes is often how we react. My friends whose parents are deep into dementia try to maintain patience amidst the constant repeating of questions and answers. It's a tough job: 59 percent of dementia caregivers rate the emotional stress of caregiving as high or very high.[2] It's difficult to treat our elders with dignity when they're driving us crazy.

I was used to relating to my dad as a father, a respected equal, and even a friend. We talked politics, religion, books, friends, and work. As his personality changed, I struggled to navigate the maze of his pain to find the father I knew. I'd like to say I was gracious, loving, and kind in the midst of my father's trial. But I'd be lying. I struggled just to be civil. I turned my face, hoping the bogeyman would go away. I could have been more patient with my dad. I could have entered into his suffering as we're told in 2 Timothy 2:3, "Share in suffering as a good soldier of Christ Jesus" (ESV).

But I couldn't accept my dad's downward tumble into old age. It seemed to have happened overnight, though in reality it happened over the course of a few years. Perhaps if someone had shown me what to expect, I would have learned earlier to rely more fully on God's grace.

Paul tells us in 1 Corinthians 13:4, "Love is patient." I've often asked the Lord to give me patience. His answer? "I've given you all the gifts, patience included. Use what I've given you." After experiencing my dad's decline, I've learned to be more patient and look less at the inconvenience others cause me. For instance,

I know my mom hates to impose by asking me to take her somewhere, especially if I have to take time off work. Transporting her is almost as much of a physical exercise as wrestling with my dad's wheelchair. Mom has one of those super-walkers, complete with brakes and a seat. I have to walk her to the car, her fingers clutching my arm like the talons of a bird of prey. When we reach the car, she pries them off while carefully stepping from the curb and struggling into the car, apologizing all the way.

I wheel the walker around to the back of the car, fold it up, and stow it away. Mom always asks, "Can you get that okay, with your hands?" What she means is, "I know you have limited mobility in your fingers and wrists because of chronic rheumatoid arthritis." She knows it's painful for me to lift her walker into the back of the Jeep. But I'm willing to do it because it's for her.

MOURNING LOSSES

Why was my attitude with my mom different from how I dealt with my dad? It's because I began to face the new reality that life was different, and it included accepting losses for my parents and for me. In his book *Hope for the Caregiver*, Peter Rosenberger says: "Life has a way of unfolding, not as we will, but as it will. And sometimes, there is precious little we can do to change things."[3]

Your new role of caregiver may look different from mine. Your loved one may have different losses to face. Whatever the situation is, talk with your parents about what they're feeling. Listening to them and acknowledging their losses will validate their emotions in this stage of life and show them that you value them, even in old age.

It's important at this point to remind them of your care. When my mother frets over what will happen when she can no longer live on her own, I promise her again that Mike and I will take care of her. Whether that means moving her into our home or visiting her every day at a nursing facility, we will be there for her. Your parent may have the same fears:

What will happen to me?

Who will take care of me?

What if . . . ?

Yet my parents weren't the only ones to experience loss in this caregiving season. I found it helpful to make a list of what *I* had lost as my parents aged. My dad's cheerful personality, going to the movies with my mom, control over my coveted time, and serendipitous trips to the mountains were some things I mourned. After writing everything down, I gave it to the Lord and asked Him to do His work in making beauty from ashes. As I opened my hands and my heart, God dropped something into my spirit that had only been in my head—that life isn't about me. The world doesn't revolve around my time, my needs, and my wants. What a unique privilege to grow into God's grace and help your aging loved ones grow too.

Although caring for my father as his personality changed would eventually remake a portion of my own character, it wasn't an easy lesson. As the father I knew began to disappear, my world changed, and facing that new reality was difficult to accept.

Grace Growers

1. Read Ecclesiastes 3:4. Make a list of your losses. Take time to consider everything you feel you've given up because of this caregiving season. Spend time with God, allowing Him

to help you mourn. If possible, ask your elderly loved one if he or she is willing to list the losses that aging has brought. Pray with your parent and validate those losses. Later, encourage your loved one to write a list of blessings, too.

2. Meditate on Philippians 4:13: "I can do all things through Christ who strengthens me" (NKJV). What are three major tasks you're facing this week that you need strength for? Take time to make your needs known to someone who cares for you.

3. Consider 2 Corinthians 12:9: "But he said to me, 'My grace is sufficient for you, for my power is made perfect in weakness.' Therefore I will boast all the more gladly of my weaknesses, so that the power of Christ may rest upon me" (ESV). How can you practically apply this verse to your situation? Can you see yourself as a receiver of God's grace and power, rather than a victim of your circumstances?

4
CALLING 9-1-1 AGAIN

Truth is like the sun. You can shut it out for a time,
but it ain't goin' away.

ELVIS PRESLEY

The phone's shrill tone dragged me from a deep sleep. Momentarily disoriented, I watched Mike grab the phone off the nightstand.

"Hullo," he mumbled.

Since I could hear only one side of the conversation, which was mercifully short, I pestered him the minute he hung up.

He groaned, rolling over to crawl out of bed. "Dad fell down in the bathroom and is stuck."

I placed my hand over my adrenaline-laced heart and watched as Mike pulled on a pair of jeans and sneakers. "I'll be back in a minute."

I lay down, staring at the dark ceiling, anxiously waiting for Mike's return. What happened this time?

How many similar calls had we answered? Along with the

middle-of-the-night calls, there were the middle-of-the-day calls, not to mention those that came while we watched a movie, ate dinner, or fellowshipped with friends.

Mike returned after thirty minutes. "That was a chore," he sighed as he undressed and climbed back into bed. "Dad was wedged between the toilet and the tub. I had a hard time getting him up without hurting him. He'll be black and blue tomorrow."

"But he's okay?"

"As okay as he's going to be at this point."

We finally got back to sleep, but the peace wouldn't last. In the morning, a fresh wave of realization hit me. Dad was not going to get better.

AVOID DENIAL

Denial is a comfortable place to reside. Denial kept me from thinking things would get worse. Most of the time in my experience, people got sick and then they got better. Diagnosed with cancer at age thirty-five, I had an operation, went through radiation, and was eventually declared cancer free. When our son, Bobby, had cancer at seventeen, he had chemo, radiation, and, voilà, was in remission. I wanted to believe my dad's situation would have the same outcome. I was like the kid who doesn't want to hear her parent. She sticks her fingers in her ears, saying, "La, la, la."

Mike, Mom, and I had never talked about what we'd do if Dad continued to lose his balance. We didn't discuss what would happen if Dad broke a hip in one of the falls. Meanwhile, Mom lost sleep listening for Dad in the middle of the night. She'd wake up when he went to the bathroom, trying to remain calm and not worry, and then go back to sleep. But her blood pressure rose every night. She became short-tempered with everyone, including Dad.

I'd get a burst of adrenaline every time the phone rang and the caller ID showed my parents' number. I'd brace myself for the worst. Had he fallen? Had a stroke? Another heart attack? I had difficulty concentrating at work since I was always on edge.

SEEK COUNSEL

I wish we'd had someone to counsel us. We were in a tiny boat in a roiling sea with no land in sight. We reacted to every event, doing what was necessary to handle the situation. Instead of looking ahead to preventive measures, like the eventuality of moving Dad to a care home, or hiring round-the-clock care, we used a "Band-Aid" to cover a gaping "wound."

If I had shared my anxiety with someone skilled to deal with such issues, I could have come to grips with my changing role. Looking back, I now know that there are many helpful resources available, locally and nationwide. (See "Suggested Resources" at the end of this book.) I learned months later that my physician keeps a list of eldercare advocates who will assess a situation and direct a caregiver in the right direction.

Although my dad didn't need constant monitoring, we should have been able to look up out of the morass to options that would be healthy for everyone. Since I was firmly in the grip of denial, I never thought about trying to climb out of the tossing boat. I'd adjusted to this new normal. Dad fell down, Mike picked him up. If Mike wasn't available, Mom called 9-1-1.

Circumstances finally forced us out of the boat. Mom called one evening to let us know Dad had fallen again. Dad had gained so much weight from fluid retention that this time, Mike couldn't lift him. We called 9-1-1. Again. Emergency personnel had already been to the house several times in the previous two months. One time, Dad couldn't breathe. Another time he was burning up with fever from a kidney infection. It had been a round-robin of trips to the emergency room, a one- or two-night hospital stay, and then bringing Dad back home, only to start the cycle again in a couple of weeks.

> God's grace is not given to make us feel better,
> but to glorify Him. . . . Good feelings may
> come, or they may not, but that is not the issue.
> The issue is whether or not we honor God by
> the way we respond to our circumstances.
> **JERRY BRIDGES**
> Author

I remember watching Dad's face during one of the emergency calls. He'd been lifted onto the gurney. One strapping young EMT checked his vitals while the other wrote information on a steel-backed clipboard. Dad's face was a placid mask of self-satisfaction. Was he actually enjoying the attention?

This time the ambulance crew showed up and greeted my parents by name. This is not a good sign. After they helped Dad back into his bed, they went to work making sure he was no worse for the fall. While they checked him, the supervisor strode from the bedroom to the living room where we waited. He held a bottle of port wine in his hand.

"Did you know your husband had this by the bed?" he asked Mom with a stern voice.

Mom's hands flew to her mouth. "No!" she exclaimed. I knew she was lying. She justified Dad's midnight nipping on the bottle by calling it "liquid pain relief."

The supervisor walked to the kitchen sink and poured the remaining liquid down the drain. Then he returned to the living room and addressed my mother.

"Mrs. Gaugler, I have to let you know that we can't continue to come here and pick up your husband every time he falls." He went on to say he'd be forced to alert Social Services if we continued to call 9-1-1, especially in light of the wine he found.

After the crew left, Mike, Mom, and I stared wordlessly at each other. What should we do? Mom was hesitant to deny Dad the little bit of comfort he received from his port. I had no answer to her dilemma.

My friend told me she experienced the same emergency room cycle with her mother-in-law. The woman had edema in her ankles and feet, causing discomfort ranging from throbbing to excruciating pain. She'd insist on being taken to the hospital. Each time, she was sent home with the same advice: lose weight, cut out sodium, and get out and walk. My friend's mother-in-law refused to change. They had come to know the ER nurses by name, just as I had with my dad.

I tried reaching out to Dad, but he was unresponsive. His stern German father had instilled a deep reserve. Dad couldn't talk about feelings or emotions. What is it about the aging process that keeps some people from reaching out for help?

"Seniors, especially men, won't admit they need help," says Flora Maloney, director of the Rancho Cordova Adult Day Care Center. "They don't want to seem vulnerable."[1]

Years later, I can look back and see that my dad's deep need to be with people wasn't being met. He used to have friends everywhere, and if he went somewhere where he didn't know anyone, he made a new friend. He once told me his reason for existing was to help others. But the constant pain accompanying his later years kept him from being able to enjoy the company of other people. I think that's why he loved seeing the EMTs and going to the hospital. He liked the attention, even though it was uncomfortable.

Tunnel vision kept me from seeing the big picture. So focused on moving from one disaster to the next, I couldn't lift my head to see my dad's greater need. Although he suffered pain from neuropathy, he still needed social contact. It was difficult to get past his misery, to see him as someone craving distraction from his pain.

LOOK AT THE HEART

I wish I could have a do-over. I now realize that Dad was grieving the loss of his vitality. He couldn't drive, and eventually couldn't take care of some of his most basic needs. He must have been deeply embarrassed to have Mike pick him up from a fall and put him back to bed. I wish I could have seen past his pain and into his heart. It brings to mind the verse in 1 Samuel 16:7: "The LORD does not look at the things man looks at. Man looks at the outward appearance, but the LORD looks at the heart."

I'd like to think I'm learning how to see people as Christ does, as His beloved children, no matter what their age. As caregivers, we're called upon to see ourselves as more than our parents' children. We're now their companions. We're their partners in navigating this "new normal." How we respond to their needs and their losses requires a full dose of grace.

Prepare yourself for your new role by learning as much as you can about options for care as well as the condition of your parents' hearts. Don't gravitate toward denial as I did. There are many resources available. If you don't know where to start, ask your family physician and locate your local Area Agency on Aging, a government-funded agency that coordinates senior programs and services in your area. I found it reassuring to join an online caregiver support group and know that others felt the same as I did.

Most of all, know that you are not alone in this journey. The Lord is by your side, girding you up and strengthening you, if you let Him.

Grace Growers

1. List the differences between your parents' lives now and their lives before their decline. Ask the Lord to show you their hearts. How can you minister to them physically and spiritually?

2. Think about the top four things you enjoy doing. What if you could no longer do them? Talk with your parents about the things *they* can no longer enjoy. Is there a way you can help your parents recover any of these joys?

3. Consider what author Jerry Bridges said about grace. What issues may you need to face as your parents age and your circumstances change? How will you respond?

5

GETTING OLD IS MESSY

Love that goes upward is worship. Love that goes
outward is affection. Love that stoops is grace.

DONALD GREY BARNHOUSE,
PASTOR AND BIBLICAL SCHOLAR

I t was a perfect September morning. The crisp, blue sky and
fluffy clouds beckoned us to the mountains. Mike and I had
promised to get my folks out of the house for a drive to Lake
Tahoe, about ninety minutes away.

We'd been on the road for approximately twenty minutes
when my dad announced he had to use the bathroom. Mike saw
a fast-food place at the next exit, so he pulled off the freeway,
lifted Dad's walker out of the back of the Jeep, and helped him
into the restroom. After he returned to the car to wait, we talked
about what we'd do once we reached the beautiful alpine lake
and resort area. Mom's enthusiasm for the trip filled the car with
joyful anticipation.

After about ten minutes, Mom asked Mike to check on Dad.
Mike came back to the car, letting us know that Dad was okay.

We talked some more and people-watched, until Mom asked Mike to check on Dad again. Mike was gone for a good twenty minutes. Mom and I wondered what could be taking so long. Had Dad fallen? Was he sick? What was happening?

Another ten minutes went by, and then Mike and Dad pushed through the restaurant door and headed to the car. As Mike folded up the walker and loaded it in the back end of the Jeep, Dad struggled into his seat.

"We have to go home," Dad announced.

Mom looked at me with dismay. "Why? What's wrong?"

Dad refused to answer.

"There was a little accident in the bathroom. We'll discuss it later," Mike said. I knew from his tone that there would be more explanation once we were home.

Mom's disappointment was palpable, and silence reigned on the drive back home. We dropped my parents off at their front door and promised Mom we'd try again in a couple of weeks. Shoulders slumped, she closed the door.

When we were alone, Mike explained that the problem was diarrhea. It had messed Dad's Depends and leaked through to his slacks. He didn't have another pad with him, and it was impossible for him to completely clean himself.

I don't know who I felt sorrier for, Mom or Dad.

IT'S PERSONAL

Incontinence is almost an expected outcome of getting old. It seems that way, with the booming sales of adult incontinence aids. For elderly adults on a fixed income, this expense is difficult to absorb. For family caregivers, it's an additional cost of caring. It's estimated the cost can be up to $1,000 per adult user per year.

Imagine the embarrassment of having your adult child clean you after an accident. It's one thing to change your baby's diaper. It's quite another to change your father's or mother's incontinence aid.

How do we gracefully honor our parents when their needs are achingly personal? I recently read a twist to the Golden Rule: Do unto others as you would have others do to your children. How tenderly my parents treated my kids whenever they babysat. They never shamed the kids for messing their diapers, nor did they scold them when they had an accident during the potty-training years.

I wish I had been prepared for my dad's physical decline. I shouldn't have been embarrassed to discuss this sensitive issue with my parents, and to encourage them to see their doctor. Discussing bowel incontinence may be embarrassing, but it can provide clues to help a doctor make a diagnosis. The treatment for fecal incontinence can be as simple as using medication like Imodium to keep the stool more solid.[1]

I'm sure my dad must have felt shame in knowing he couldn't control his bodily functions. It was another inexorable step toward total dependence on others. What would be next? Having to be fed? Bathed? Clothed?

I used to drive, but now I can't.

I used to be able to read, but now my eyesight is gone.

I can't hear the conversations around me. I feel isolated.

I need help getting in and out of the shower. I used to shower whenever I wanted to. Now I have to schedule it around my child's availability. It's too much of a bother.

Independence shrinks by degrees, until the senior may give up. Depression can settle in like an uninvited guest. When Dad's health went downhill, so did his ability to focus outwardly and be his usual generous self. He focused all his attention on himself. His conversation sounded like this: *When is dinner? How long until I can have more pain meds? I need to go to the store now. How long will the doctor make me wait? Why can't I . . . bathe myself . . . go to the bathroom by myself . . . cut my own food?*

I finally did some research, looking for options that would help us care for Dad. I found a local company specializing in eldercare options. The caseworker assessed Dad's condition, inspected their home, and asked many questions. Her evaluation was that Dad wasn't at the point of needing round-the-clock care. She recommended a part-time caregiver who could help

---

DEPRESSION OR NORMAL AGING?

Be aware that not all withdrawal is depression. Some studies show that as people reach old age, "interiority" can occur, in which elders lose interest in outside events and become preoccupied with themselves. "Interiority" is accepted by gerontologists as a process by which the elderly accept their losses and limitations.

It can be disconcerting, however, for an adult child who has known and respected a parent for his life passion, outgoing personality, and many interests. If your elderly loved one begins to draw the shades down on the windows to his former world, don't panic. It may be a natural preparation for leaving this life. . . . If your loved one's withdrawal is accompanied by chronic sadness and an inability to feel pleasure in any realm, seek advice from a doctor.[2]

Dad bathe and take my parents to doctors' appointments. She suggested applying for a little-known veteran's benefit called Aid and Attendance.

Although the process took several months, it was worth it. Maria, Dad's aide, became part of the family and was the only one who could coax a smile out of my father. One of Maria's duties was to change Dad's sheets if he'd had an accident. She'd help him into the shower, give him a few minutes of privacy to wash, and then be back to help him dry off and dress.

My friend Kim told me she sets a clean Depends on the bathroom counter every morning so her mother-in-law will remember to change it. At ninety-four years old, Lil can't get out of bed in the middle of the night, so the Depends keeps her from having an accident. She wears one during the day as well. She doesn't get around as easily as she used to. Sometimes she forgets to take it off and put on a clean one in the morning. Lil may shuffle to the breakfast table, the sharp smell of urine permeating the room. Kim patiently tells Lil to go to the bathroom and change.

After a lengthy illness, my mom contracted C.diff, short for clostridium difficile colitis. It's a bacterial infection that causes uncontrollable diarrhea, and it's estimated that there are almost half a million new cases of C.diff every year, mostly among the elderly and those with compromised immune systems.[3] Mom was hospitalized, but not before suffering several days at home. Her best friend stayed at Mom's house every day to clean her up and change her Depends. Understandably, Mom was too embarrassed to have Mike or me help her.

Although women have twice as many incidents of urinary incontinence, both sexes can become incontinent because of stroke, neurologic injury, and physical problems associated with aging. Incontinence occurs in up to 30 percent of the community-dwelling elderly and 50 percent of the elderly in long-term care.[4]

GIVE THEM GRACE

The Bible says in John 21:18, "I tell you the truth, when you were younger you dressed yourself and went where you wanted; but when you are old you will stretch out your hands, and someone else will dress you." Although Jesus was talking to Peter about the kind of death he would have, it reminds me of watching my parents age. Not only do they need intimate care for their bowel and bladder issues, they also need a steady shoulder to rest on.

Thank the Lord, our hope is in more than just this life and its inconveniences. Christians have the advantage of being able to take the long view. We have the eternal perspective of heaven in the future, which is a helpful reminder to me and to my parents that there's more to life than this current difficult season.

We also have God's grace in the present—and its power. In Romans 15:15–16, Paul speaks of "the grace God gave me to be a minister of Christ Jesus to the Gentiles." God can also give you the grace and strength to honor your loved one, even when the circumstances are uncomfortable.

John Piper, founder of desiringGod.org and chancellor of Bethlehem College & Seminary, notes the connection between grace, power, and strength.

"Grace is not simply leniency when we have sinned. Grace is the enabling gift of God not to sin. Grace is power, not just pardon. . . .Therefore the effort we make to obey God is not an effort done in our own strength, but 'in the strength which

God supplies, that in everything God may get the glory' (1 Peter 4:11)."[5]

Remember, God has an unlimited supply of strength, and He is ready to give it to you. As you deal with your parent's changing circumstances, keep in mind Psalm 68:35: "You are awesome, O God, in your sanctuary; the God of Israel gives power and strength to his people. Praise be to God!"

Grace Growers

1. Discuss with your loved one, as you are comfortable, the subject of bowel or bladder control. Try to take a matter-of-fact approach to the subject, letting your parent know that there may be medical or practical help for the situation.
2. Did you know that hospitals, universities, and some companies make use of high-tech "old-age suits" so health care workers and manufacturers can better understand how it feels to be elderly? These suits have goggles to simulate poor vision, headphones to replicate hearing loss, gloves that make the hands shake, and vests that cause slouching. The suits also feature shoes that cause shuffling and braces to prevent easy movement.[6] Wearing one of these suits helps people have empathy for the elderly. Can you put on your own "old-age suit" to increase your empathy for your parent? Mentally trade places with your aging loved one as you consider his or her daily life. How would you want to be treated?

6

HOW TO SAY GOOD-BYE

He will wipe every tear from their eyes. There will
be no more death or mourning or crying or pain,
for the old order of things has passed away.

REVELATION 21:4

Sometimes it seems as if life's downpours lead only to monsoons. As Dad's health continued to deteriorate, the number of falls, trips to the emergency room, and stays in the hospital multiplied. He eventually progressed to a wheelchair.

When the EMT talked about calling a social worker, I panicked. I didn't want a social worker making decisions for my dad. I would handle this, just as I'd handled every crisis we'd experienced in the prior months. I was super-daughter. I would be my dad's savior, instead of letting the real Savior do His work. Perhaps a social worker could have shown us how to navigate the murky waters of a loved one's decline. Social workers offer counseling as a way to find solutions to a family's concerns. Instead of stopping and taking time to pray, I jumped ahead of God. I could have moved forward with godly wisdom, not human ability.

I called the eldercare caseworker again. She met with us, asked dozens more questions, and delivered her recommendation: Dad couldn't live at home anymore. She suggested we look at a few group homes that specialized in eldercare. We found a nice, family-run care home a few miles from where we lived.

The next time the caseworker came to the house, we were armed with facts about why my father needed to make this move. Yet, the facts couldn't shield my heart from having to tell Dad that he couldn't live at home anymore. He would no longer be able to wake up every morning next to Charleen, his wife of more than sixty years. He couldn't prepare the coffee at night for breakfast the next morning. There would be no more helping Mom by setting the table or emptying the dishwasher. His world would shrink to a seven-by-ten-foot bedroom.

As difficult as it was telling Dad he couldn't drive, this was worse. We let the eldercare advocate take the lead.

"Roger, I'm concerned about your safety and your overall health."

Dad nodded. I don't think he knew where this conversation was headed.

"Charleen can't keep calling 9-1-1 when you fall. You know she's not strong enough to pick you up, right?"

Dad murmured agreement.

"You have a couple of options I'd like to talk about."

She first suggested that he could have someone move in to offer around-the-clock care. Dad looked at Mom. "How do you feel about that?"

Mom shook her head. "I'm not comfortable with it. I don't want a stranger in our house."

"Your second option is to move to a place where you'll have more hands-on care," the eldercare worker told my father.

Dad visibly recoiled. "If I have to go into a convalescent hospital, I'll stop taking my meds and *die*." After one particularly nasty fall, he'd been hospitalized and then released to a convalescent hospital. He hated it.

The advocate nodded with understanding. "I know, but that's not what I'm talking about. Are you familiar with a board-and-care home?"

She explained he'd be in a home environment, with his own room. A full-time caretaker would fix meals, help with bathing, and assist with any mobility issues.

I squirmed in my chair as she moved the conversation from "if" to "when." Guilt and grief in equal measure washed over me. I couldn't breathe. As I stepped outside to try to regain equilibrium, my cell phone rang. It was my daughter, Heather, calling to see how the conversation was going.

"This is the most difficult thing I've ever had to do," I told her. "How can we make your grandpa move somewhere else?" It was like putting a child up for adoption. Or shoving my dad onto the streets. How could I force him to live with *strangers*?

Dad seemed resigned to the move. Mom cried, already grieving the separation. I was still focused on my angst over having the dreaded conversation with Dad. I had little empathy for my mom, who'd been able to wake up next to the same man for the past sixty-plus years.

As stressful as the situation was, my dad's move to the board-and-care home was the best decision for both my parents. We found a lovely home in a woodsy neighborhood run by a Russian woman who oversaw the six residents. Dad took some familiar things with him, including his television, and we borrowed many old movies from the library. For a time, he seemed to thrive. My mom got more rest as well, since she didn't wake up every time Dad got up in the middle of the night. Mike or I drove Mom to visit Dad every day after work. On the weekends, we'd drop her off for a lengthy visit.

FACING DEATH

After five months in the care home, things changed for the worse. Dad was too sick to visit our family doctor for a follow-up appointment regarding the results of his kidney function test. I happened to be at that same doctor's office for a physical, so I asked for the results to pass along to my folks. The doctor patted my shoulder as he gave me my dad's death sentence.

"His kidneys are failing, and he will slowly decline over the next ten days or so."

How do I tell my dad he's dying? What words could soften the knife-thrust of the phrase, "You only have about two weeks to live"? Mike, Mom, and I talked about what we would say. This wasn't something we could communicate without showing a united front. Mom wasn't emotionally capable of telling Dad by herself.

I'm grateful for a wonderful husband. Mike did most of the talking so Mom and I could sob quietly into our tissues. He explained that a hospice worker would come to see Dad by the end of the week.

"And she'll help me get better, right?" Dad asked.

The three of us shook our heads like pendulums. "No, Dad," I said. "She's going to talk to you about the dying process."

"She'll bring some medicine to help me get better, right?" Dad asked.

My stomach clenched. Dad wasn't getting it. "No, Dad. There isn't any medicine," I told him. "Your kidneys are failing. The doctor wants you to be prepared."

As I tried to pull Dad from the grasp of denial, I also dealt with my desire to ignore reality. I wanted my dad back, the way he was in the years before he grew old. I wanted him to come to my house, sit at my table, and drink coffee with me. I wanted him to pick me up at work at lunchtime and take me to Taco Bell or Arby's.

Gerald Sittser, in *A Grace Disguised*, says, "We are deceived by our longings for what we once had, because we cannot have it that way forever, even if we regain what we lost for a while."[1] Dad would eventually die, and I needed to face that fact.

My prayer changed from asking for Dad's healing to begging God for Dad's salvation. We'd had many conversations about Jesus, and Dad always said he didn't believe. Mike talked to him, Mom encouraged him, but Dad was polite and stoic in his rebuffs.

I was twenty-one before God became real to me. From then on, my life radically changed for the better. Once I made the

---

You are now forced to cope with the loss of parental love and attention that was given, uniquely, to you, and that you depended on, possibly even took for granted.

CAROL STAUDACHER
Author of *Beyond Grief*

decision to turn my life over to Christ, I told my family about my beliefs. Mom was enthusiastic, Dad only marginally so.

"That's great, Chickie. Glad it works for you."

I never understood how Dad could have taught Sunday school in the Methodist Church in his younger years, and still deny his need for the Savior of the world.

Once the death sentence was real, Mike and I made even more of an effort to witness to Dad. We asked him time and time again what he thought would happen to him after he died. He answered, "I'll take my chances."

Ten days later, as he ate his dinner, Dad began struggling for breath. The hospice worker called us, and we rushed over to find Dad gasping for air. I got right up to his ear and yelled, "I love you, Daddy! You need to turn to Jesus right now and be saved!" I repeated this over and over until he slipped into eternity. To our knowledge, Dad never received Christ despite our continual witness to him. I won't know until I get to heaven if he's there. I don't know if in those last moments, his spirit responded at last to the call of Christ. I hope it wasn't too late. Perhaps as he came to grips with the reality of the end of his life, he made the decision quietly in his heart.

It's hard watching your parent die. Our American culture keeps us from looking closely at dying. In movies, death is depicted as a peaceful passing. The Hollywood, sanitized version doesn't show the indignities associated with the dying process. You never see a dying person filling her adult diaper because she can't hold her bowels. They don't show an elderly man lying helpless on the floor, wetting himself because he can't get to the bathroom. Rarely depicted is a man or woman writhing in pain from inoperable cancer.

Yet this is as much a part of life as the beauty of birth. Death is ugly. Death steals our humanity and our dignity. We were never created to die. When God created Adam and Eve in the Garden of Eden, He meant for them to live forever, infinite like Himself. Their sin brought death into the world, and to every descendant. Thank God for Jesus, who conquered death so we no longer have to fear it.

Our suffering is just for a little while. We can have this assurance from 2 Corinthians 4:16–17: "Therefore we do not lose heart, but though our outer man is decaying, yet our inner man is being renewed day by day. For momentary, light affliction is producing for us an eternal weight of glory far beyond all comparison" (NASB). If my dad had known Jesus, he would have been able to see beyond the indignity of his physical limitations. He would have known that soon he'd shed this finite body for the infinite.

Although it was exhausting caring for my dad as his needs grew, I would gladly do it again if it meant having him here again for a little while. As you grow weary in caregiving, remember that this is a season. Seasons change, and your elderly loved one will eventually pass out of this life. Enjoy your parent's presence while you can.

While Dad was in the board-and-care home, we had the joy of talking about his childhood. Although he didn't have loving and affectionate parents, he loved to talk about growing up on a working farm. He and his siblings rode horses, milked cows, and learned to work on farm machinery. He always mentioned the grapes they grew.

"They were as big as ping-pong balls," he'd tell us.

Even if we'd heard the stories umpteen times, we'd still ask.

Sometimes Mom chimed in and talked about their early married life. Showing an interest in your loved ones' early memories creates a legacy of stories to pass down to children and grandchildren. I'm glad we took the time to relive happy memories from Dad's past.

Dad was eighty-nine when he died. The funeral home where we had the service set up chairs for thirty-five people. We figured most people who knew him had already passed. We were shocked when more than twice as many people as expected attended his service. People were shoulder-to-shoulder, standing around the edges of the room. Dad would have loved it.

After all the busyness surrounding Dad's death and memorial service died down, the focus of my worry shifted to my mom. How could I carry my grief and help her carry hers? Dinners with Mike, me, and Mom often found us crying into our food. We talked about how much we missed Dad. Talking about Dad seemed to help my mom grieve.

BE PREPARED

One thing I learned after watching my father's health disintegrate was to have an open discussion with my mom about how she wants to age. My dad's situation caught me off guard. I thought he would die peacefully in his sleep, with no lessening of his vitality.

Several months after Dad died, I began to talk to Mom about what we should do when she could no longer live alone. Should she move in with Mike and me? Or should we move in with her? Would she move to an assisted-living facility?

In our culture we shy away from frank discussions about death, even though humans have a 100 percent mortality rate.

"As frightening and painful as it can be, if your loved one is aging, you should consider talking to him about death before it's too late," writes Connie Matthiessen in a Caring.com article. "By avoiding the topic, you could be depriving him—and yourself— of the opportunity to share this final life transition."[2]

Experts suggest looking for natural openings to begin these conversations, such as following a funeral or when your parent mentions her mortality or a friend's passing. If your loved one begins talking about his or her own death, just try to listen, suggests Matthiessen. She continues,

> It can be tempting to jump in with reassuring words like, "Now, Dad, I'm sure it's not that bad!" . . . Such reactions reflect your own natural desire to protect him, and yourself, from painful feelings. But downplaying the situation won't help him come to terms with his own passing or make him feel comfortable sharing it with you. Instead, try to let him express all his feelings. . . . Talk about your own grief, feelings, and memories, and let him know that he's loved and that you'll do your best to support him throughout the process.[3]

Families also need to discuss practical matters before it's too late. "We have many clients in their mid-sixties who have Alzheimer's disease set in, or have a stroke," says Dick Edwards, author of *Mom, Dad . . . Can We Talk?* "It leaves the family in a state of confusion and with a lot of guilt because they're then not sure if they're doing what Mom and Dad wish."[4] Finding the answers to these questions is beneficial for all involved:

> Do your parents have an advance directive (also known as a living will)? It's important that you know how they wish to be treated during the dying process and after death.
> What final arrangements do they want, and how should they be paid for?
> How does your parent envision the memorial service? Are there special songs or Scriptures he or she would like included?
> Do your parents have a will, trusts, or special bequests?
> What plans have been made for the surviving spouse?
> Are life insurance beneficiaries up-to-date?
> What financial accounts do they have, and where are they?
> Where are the tax files, and do they have a safety deposit box and key?

While it's easier to turn away from the elephant in the room (the fact that your parents' days are becoming fewer), it won't stop the inevitable from happening. As difficult as it is to talk about death and dying, there is hope for the believer. You may find it helpful to focus on the eternal perspective and to encourage your loved one to do so also. Consider reading portions of Scripture together that talk about eternal life. John 14:2–3 says, "In my Father's house are many rooms; if it were not so, I would have told you. I am going there to prepare a place for you. And if I go and prepare a place for you, I will come back and take you to be with me that you also may be where I am."

Grace Growers

1. What would help your loved one prepare for his or her passing? If you can, ask your parent how you may help.
2. Talk to your loved one about heaven. How does she picture it? Share some verses from Scripture about life after death and the description of heaven. Make a list of people your loved one is looking forward to seeing on the other side.
3. Meditate on John 14:2–3. Think about how you prepare your home for visitors and guests.
4. Now think about Jesus, preparing His home for your parent. Share this with your loved one if possible.

PART II

BARGAINING WITH GRACE

7

MAY I BE FRANK?

A man can no more take in a supply of grace
for the future than he can eat enough for the
next six months, or take sufficient air into his
lungs at one time to sustain life for a week.
We must draw upon God's boundless store of
grace from day to day, as we need it.

D.L. MOODY, EVANGELIST

"What time do you leave for work in the morning?"
It's 7:30 at night, and my mom has called to ask me a seemingly innocuous question.

"Usually around 8:00 or so." My hand grips the phone, waiting for the sucker punch.

"Oh," she says, with a sigh.

The silence lengthens. I'm determined to wait her out. My fingers drum on the countertop as I squeeze my eyes shut and inhale. I feel my mouth open as the words rush out. "Why do you want to know?"

"I made some muffins for Dr. B's staff, and I need to have

them dropped off. I thought you could do it on your way to work."

"Dr. B's office doesn't open until 8:30."

"I know."

"I have to be at work at 8:30."

"Oh." She's waiting for me to say I'll go in late. I grit my teeth. *I won't give in. I won't give in. I won't give in.*

Mom sighs. "I guess I'll get Dodie to do it." Dodie is her friend and errand runner.

I exhale. I've dodged a bullet. I set a boundary and stuck by it.

Sometimes I wonder if the boundaries I set are my selfishness bubbling to the surface. Could I be five or ten minutes late for work? Yes. Would my world come crashing down if I did this one small favor? Maybe not, but it would be easier if this "one small favor" wasn't repeated several times a week. I grow weary of the assaults on my time. I see it this way: I've budgeted my time, and Mom is constantly trying to exceed her portion of my budget.

Conversations like these occur at regular intervals; some of them take place every day. They range from "When will you be going to the grocery store?" to "Are you busy Tuesday?" There's an ulterior motive behind every question. Sometimes I wish for a phone call just to ask how I'm doing, or how my day was.

As an elderly person's world shrinks, her needs often increase. She may no longer have a supportive spouse to lean on. No one is there to fix the leaky faucet, change the out-of-reach lightbulb, or take out the garbage. No one is constantly nearby, ready to listen to worries and give assurance or attention. This can often lead to multiple requests lobbed at a son or daughter, who is often at a loss about how to handle the onslaught.

FEELING MANIPULATED

In my mother's case, instead of healthy, direct, and loving interactions such as asking, "Will you please...," she brings her requests through the back door, and I end up feeling manipulated. She doesn't want to be a burden so she beats around the bush, hoping I'll respond without her having to ask. Perhaps she's afraid of my rejection, or that I'll become exasperated with her and her world will shrink even further.

My mom called all the shots in my parents' sixty-plus years of marriage. My dad was a lot like me. We're pretty easygoing until we get our backs up. Then it's like trying to take down a thirty-inch-thick concrete wall. We don't move. My dad experienced a lot of yelling and fighting in his growing-up years, so he let my mom steer the boat. I think Mom is so used to getting her own way, she doesn't know what to do when she's stonewalled.

Using manipulation is simply a way to control your world, and I have certainly employed this technique. As a child, I dropped subtle hints about upcoming events that I very much wanted to attend. Only after several days of hinting would I come right out and ask, "What do you think about me going to Susan's party?"

I also used reverse psychology to get my son to do something he didn't want to do. All I had to do was tell him he wasn't allowed to do it. He'd immediately take the opposite stance. I learned to manipulate around his strong will.

No one wants to feel manipulated. Asking God to help us address these situations in a godly way is necessary to avoid long-term feelings of resentment that can ruin a relationship.

In addition to feeling manipulated, we can also feel flummoxed by our parents' attempts to keep secrets. I've heard many stories of elderly parents controlling what their children see. It might sound like this:

"Don't look there, look over here." *I spilled something and I don't want you to see it.*

"Come over this way, honey." *Look at my new blouse, not at the one I burned on the stovetop from getting too close.*

"Don't go into the kitchen . . . it's a mess." *Because I put something metal in the microwave and it blew up.*

"Come sit down on the sofa." *Not at the dining room table . . . I haven't moved the last six weeks of newspapers to the recycle bin.*

Elderly parents sometimes keep secrets because they feel their independence slipping away. According to Agingcare.com, "They might be embarrassed to ask for help. They might fear their family's reaction. They might be afraid that family members will 'put them away.' Or they simply might not want help," the article explains. "So they cover up bruises, falls, car accidents, money trouble, alcohol use, and more."[1]

FAILURE TO COMMUNICATE

Yet disagreements with our elderly parents may have nothing to do with their desire to maintain control or keep secrets. Sometimes arguments result from poor communication. We may simply need to express our needs and schedules, and then seek an option that will work for everyone. Could it be that even as adult children, we still feel the need to immediately please our parents without looking for other solutions?

One friend said his mom waits until the last minute to inform him of a doctor's appointment. His job is more flexible than his wife's is, so he has more of the caretaking role.

"I have to go to the doctor today," his mother will say.

"Mom, I can't take you today. Is there any way you can reschedule?"

"No, it has to be today. It's the only time the specialist is available."

This goes back and forth for a few minutes until my friend capitulates. "Fine. I'll rearrange my schedule for you." Meanwhile, he's screaming inside from frustration and feels manipulated.

"Have you thought about talking to your mother about your schedule at the beginning of the week?" I asked him. "Maybe if she knows what appointments you have, she'd be willing to work around them."

He told me later that my suggestion seems to be working.

> **Old age comes on suddenly, and
> not gradually as is thought.**
> **EMILY DICKINSON**

In other situations, feelings of "being invisible" may be at the root of an impasse. One day, my mom asked Mike to figure out why her alarm pad was chirping. They ended up in an argument over which code, or area, had caused the chirp. Mom insisted it was one thing, Mike insisted it was something else. Mike was right.

After fixing the problem, Mike sat down across the kitchen table from Mom.

"I'm sorry," he began. "I don't like to argue with you like this."
Mom's eyes filled with tears.

"Why were you so insistent?" Mike asked.

"I don't want to talk about it," she answered.

"Is it because you don't like being wrong?"

Finally Mom opened up. "I just feel like no one listens to me because I'm old."

Mike said that he learned a lesson that day on how to listen before insisting on being right.

"The number one complaint of older people, regardless of where they live, is that 'nobody listens to me anymore,'" says David Oliver. "Yet the way we are accorded value and worth is to have someone listen to and care about what we have to say."[2]

Somehow, we must step through the frustrations of caregiving and into our parents' shoes, reminding ourselves that Mom or Dad is also a person struggling through a challenging phase of life that we have yet to experience. It's difficult, yet imperative, to step out of the role of child as we interact with our elderly loved ones. Frank, open discussions about needs, desires, schedules, and availability have to happen if we're to care for our parents with grace.

GOING TO GOD

These types of honest discussions are important, yet at the same time, God reminds me to hold loosely to my own desires. According to 1 Corinthians 13:5, love does not dishonor others, and it is not self-seeking. Meditating on this verse, I'm reminded once again to honor my father and my mother. Can I sacrifice my time? How much time did my dad sacrifice for me, taking me to a friend's house, picking me up late, teaching me to drive?

I think about my mom, helping me shop for school clothes and fulfilling all the items on my birthday wish list. Am I willing to put aside my time budget to help pay bills, pick up a prescription, or just have coffee and talk? The answer is yes. I'm willing, not because I'm paying my parents back for the things they did for me, but because of Jesus' love.

I never thought it was an inconvenience to drive my kids various places. I didn't think twice about carting them to the doctor when they were sick. I drove them to swim practice, Little League, basketball games, and friends' houses. I cooked dinner and made their brown-bag lunches for school. I did their laundry, cleaned up after them, and bandaged bloody knees.

So why do I get so annoyed when my mom needs something? Especially knowing she can't do it on her own. Perhaps I'd be more willing if I didn't feel manipulated. Maybe I'd like her to ask in a certain way for it to be okay with me.

"Jane, darling, I know you're busy. It's a lot to ask, but would you mind terribly picking up a prescription for me on your way home from work?"

Or how's this: "Jane, you've always been so good to me. I can't tell you how much I appreciate everything you're doing for me. Would it be too much to ask for you to take me to the store on Sunday? I know you're busy, and it's okay if you say no."

These thoughts would be humorous if they weren't so nauseating. When I go to God whining and complaining about how I feel manipulated, He reminds me of His grace. Because of His abundant love for me, He gave it all—His life for mine. Therefore, I have two choices. I can either give in to my flesh and lash out at my mom, or I can breathe in the Spirit of God.

As I let God's peace rest on me, I'm able to take care of my mom's needs.

The Holy Spirit has to remind me every day that Mom can't do the things she used to do. I've also had to repent of any hint that my mom's requests are an imposition. I've spoken frankly to her that I'm happy to be of service to her, and that it's okay for her to be straightforward and ask me if she needs something. And as I go to the Father, I submit my time as a sacrifice of love for my family and for Him.

Grace Growers

1. Take some time to recognize any feelings of manipulation in your relationship with your loved one. Can you have a frank talk with your parent about your feelings?

2. Meditate on Ephesians 6:12: "For our struggle is not against flesh and blood, but against the rulers, against the authorities, against the powers of this dark world and against the spiritual forces of evil in the heavenly realms." When you're tempted to argue with your loved one, remember that your struggle isn't against him or her. The Enemy would love to see you become resentful in caregiving. To avoid this, follow the instructions in James 4:7: "Submit yourselves, then, to God. Resist the devil, and he will flee from you."

8

SIBLING RIVALRY

Get rid of all bitterness, rage and anger, brawling
and slander, along with every form of malice. Be
kind and compassionate to one another, forgiving
each other, just as in Christ God forgave you.

EPHESIANS 4:31-32

"What are we going to do with Mom?"

My oldest brother's question rear-ended me. Not
only had Dean rarely called in my adult life, but now he asked a
question for which I had no ready answer.

"She shouldn't be living by herself," he insisted.

I immediately went on the defensive.

"She's fine on her own. Mike and I check on her almost
every day."

Who was he to tell me how Mom was doing? He'd been to see
her only three or four times since our dad died, four years earlier.
Who did he think he was? He'd never been available to check on
Mom while we went on vacation. He never thought of taking
Mom to lunch or dinner. Why the sudden concern?

Bonnie Lawrence of the Family Caregiver Alliance describes what I already knew. "It's determined, often by default, that one person—perhaps the one who lives the closest, or doesn't have kids, or is the oldest—will take on the role of primary caregiver," she says. "The disagreements now are over care for your parent: who does or doesn't do it; how much; who's in charge. At the same time, your parent is very aware—and most likely not happy—that he or she has become so dependent on you."[1]

One of my earliest memories is from when I was four or five years old. My grandparents often joined the five of us for dinner. I remember pointing to the carton of milk and grunting. One of the adults reached for the milk and poured some in my cup.

"Why doesn't she have to use her words?" my brother asked belligerently.

My folks shrugged. As the baby and the only girl, I got away with a lot. Another time, I was allowed to have iced tea instead of milk, much to my brother's chagrin.

"I didn't get to have iced tea at her age!"

I loved getting one over on my older brothers because they were allowed to do so much more than I was. While they stayed home alone, I had to stay at a friend's house if my folks went out. They were permitted to play with power tools and electronics, but I was too young. They climbed on the roof. The one time I did that, I was spanked.

For years I've wanted my older brother to step up and help with Mom. I've raged against the unfairness of the situation, become bitter toward him, and even cursed him. What has it gained me?

Nothing.

At some point I realized my anger can't change him and that I was only making myself miserable. I'm grateful for God's shoulders, which are big enough to carry my bitterness. As I look back on it now, I see how I have unconsciously cut Dean out of any involvement in Mom's care. I could have continued to pursue him, continued to ask, even knowing I'd be rejected every time. I could have called him every so often to let him know about upcoming doctor's appointments, any financial challenges Mom faced, or to generally update him. Perhaps I've unconsciously communicated that I don't trust him to agree with my decisions regarding Mom's care.

DON'T PLAY THE MARTYR

"If you are the primary caregiver communicating with family, express your feelings and personal needs using simple terms and few words. Avoid accusing your siblings in any way," I read in the *Complete Guide to Caring for Aging Loved Ones* by Focus on the Family. "Don't play the martyr, listing all you do for your parent or relative and expecting your viewpoints to be validated or preferred."[2]

Reading this, I had to ask myself: *Have I played the martyr before God?* As I articulate all the things I've done for my folks, I realize I sound like a whiny brat. I want Mom, my brothers, my friends, even God, to pat me on the back and say, "You're such a good daughter. And a good person, too. God bless you."

One of my parents' friends had a stroke several months ago. The daughter of this friend talked about her struggle to deal with the sibling friction as it related to their mom's care.

Should they tear down walls in their mother's home to accommodate a wheelchair?

Could they all pitch in to pay for twenty-four-hour care?
Would a board-and-care home be able to handle their mother's needs?

According to Francine Russo of Family Caregiver Alliance, siblings may be competing with each other just as they did when they were kids and not even realize it. When those old needs for parental love and approval get stirred up, sibling rivalry can reignite.

> **Siblings are so complicated. For many people they're their best friend, and for others they're their worst enemy.**
> **JONATHAN CASPI**
> Author of *Sibling Aggression*

"So when you're discussing whether Dad needs a more expensive wheelchair or Mom is still safe at home, try to keep the discussion on the concrete issue at hand, not on which of you cares the most or knows what is best," advises Russo.[3] Try to accept your siblings—and your parents—as they really are, not who you wish they were.

My brother Alan and his wife decided to move her parents, Barbara and Jack, from Oregon to an independent living facility in the Bay Area. Barbara's health had worsened, and my sister-in-law was worried about them living so far away with no family nearby.

Soon after they were settled, Barbara had a heart attack and was hospitalized. She needed immediate surgery. This so stressed

Jack that he also had a heart attack and wound up in the hospital. Weeks later, they're now back in the facility, but have lost some cognitive function. Since my brother is retired and my sister-in-law isn't, the obligation falls to him to drive thirty minutes twice a day to make sure Jack and Barbara take their medications.

A couple of weeks ago, my brother called me in a panic.

"You'll never believe where I am right now," he said.

"Umm, in Mexico?"

"If only. No, I'm in the emergency room at Stanford Hospital. I brought Barbara here to have a checkup after her heart surgery. While she was being examined, Jack thought he was having a heart attack."

"Oh, my! Was he?"

"No. Turns out it was only a panic attack, but he had to be totally checked out. I'm waiting for him now." My brother's voice was gravelly with exasperation. What he thought would be a minor checkup for his mother-in-law turned into major drama.

Although a part of me felt empathy for my brother's stress, part of me wanted to scream. *What do you think I've been dealing with for the past seven years?*

He was definitely beginning to feel my pain. If I could just get my oldest brother to . . . I wasn't sure what. Help Mom financially? Give us some respite? Visit more often? I don't know what he could do to make my burden lighter. I'm not sure what I'd consider "fair."

A NEW ATTITUDE

As I look back over the choices Mike and I have made, I take responsibility for deciding to live near my folks for most of my adult life. I chose to say yes to caregiving. No one insisted I visit my dad in the board-and-care home or cook for my mom every night. I chose this role because I love my mother. I want to be Jesus in the flesh.

In addition, God showed me it's okay to let my brothers into my world without condemnation for how much or how little involvement they have in Mom's care—and without playing the martyr. This wisdom came only after I poured out my bitterness and resentment to the Lord.

Because I've been the one to step up to meet my parents' needs, I had closed my heart to my brothers. At first I thought, *I'm the only one caring for Mom and Dad.* Somewhere along the line, my thoughts became, *I'm the only one who CAN care for Mom and Dad.* I didn't need my brothers, I didn't want my brothers, and yet I blamed them for not stepping up.

When I allowed God to reveal my attitude, I had to repent. I needed to ask my brothers to help, regardless of their response. They wouldn't know how to help unless I reached out. This was a painful lesson.

I've found it helpful having a handful of people I can share with who can listen to me and offer encouragement. It's difficult to maintain many relationships between working full time and taking care of my own home and my mom's needs. There's not a lot of spontaneity. So Mike and I consider our schedule every Sunday, deciding when we can meet with friends.

Sure, I wish our family were more like the Waltons, that old TV family with all the siblings living close by, supporting each other through every challenge. Nevertheless, God's grace has me in this family for such a time as this.

When I asked, God gave me His perspective on my relationship with my siblings. As you examine your family situation, ask God to reveal any destructive emotions you need to repent of. If needed, seek His help to "get rid of all bitterness, rage and anger," replacing it with kindness and forgiveness (Ephesians 4:31–32).

Grace Growers

1. Ask God to show you if you've slipped into the martyr role. How can you step out of that role and invite your siblings to share the responsibility for decision making and care for your elderly loved one?

2. Think about your role in the family. Are you stuck being the baby, the jokester, or the responsible one? How can you become the adult caregiver God wants you to be?

9

THE LINE IN THE SAND

You need boundaries. . . . Even in our
material creation, boundaries mark the most
beautiful of places, between the ocean and
the shore, between the mountains and the
plains, where the canyon meets the river.

WM. PAUL YOUNG, AUTHOR

I hated the boundaries my parents set for me.

"You can ride your bike as far as Adam's house, but no farther."

"Two hours at the mall is enough."

"No single dating until you're sixteen."

It seemed my brothers were allowed to do more and go farther at a much younger age than I was. My mother believed she was protecting me from the evils that can befall a young girl. Including what might happen if I wore jeans.

Even after I begged, pleaded, and threw tantrums, my mom still wouldn't budge on the jeans issue. So I bought a pair with my own money and kept them at my friend's house. I'd stop at Jan's before school, change, and then do the same thing in reverse after school. Problem solved.

If only it were that easy now. The Bible says we're to honor our parents. For a child, this means to obey them (Colossians 3:20). But when we're adult children caring for our elderly parents, we need to avoid emotionally responding to situations as a child would.

Even though I've been an adult for forty-plus years, at times I feel as if I haven't left home emotionally. I often find myself reacting as I did in the jeans incident: Rather than confront my parents, I circumvent the issue.

For example, Mom feels the need to help me control my husband's diet. He's constantly trying to lose weight, and he loves to eat. He appreciates good cooking, usually his own, and he has an insatiable sweet tooth. When he helps himself to seconds, or takes a large portion of dessert, Mom makes a comment. It's usually couched as helpful, but is no less hurtful.

"I thought you were on a diet," she'll say. Or maybe this: "Is this a cheat day?" "Are you still going to the gym?" "How many pounds did you lose last week?"

Over the past thirty-eight years, I've learned I can't control Mike's eating. He doesn't need to hear me nag, and it certainly doesn't help our relationship. And yet, rather than asking Mom to stop commenting on this, both of us ignore her barbs.

Part of me doesn't want to deal with the emotional turmoil of confronting her. I know she'll cry, and then she'll feel guilty and beat herself up. She'll be good for a few days or weeks. Then her natural tendencies will creep back like the ocean tide, blurring the line in the sand.

DRAWING THE LINE

When you're in the position of caring for your parent, it's easy to revert to being a child again, especially if your relationship was never healthy to begin with. It can be difficult to create a boundary as an adult if no boundaries previously existed. How do we draw that boundary line? Consider how my friends George and Lucy handled a similar situation.

George's mother, Elsa, lives with him and his wife, Lucy. Lucy takes the brunt of Elsa's criticism, which may sound like this:

"She's a sloppy housekeeper."

"The food she cooks is too salty."

"She doesn't do the laundry the way I like it."

George is snared like a fox in a steel trap. If he takes a stand for Lucy, he suffers the backlash from his mom. If he defends his mother to Lucy, she accuses him of choosing his mother over her.

George sought advice from his pastor, who explained to him that as our parents age they lose control of many things, including

---

When you start taking care of your parent,
they lose the one thing they've always had in
relationship to you: authority. That's not going to
be easy for them to give up. Expect them, in one
way or another, to lash out about that loss.

JOHN SHORE
"Fifteen Ways to Stay Sane While Caring
for an Elderly Parent"

---

the authority they once held. Elsa lashed out in anger at Lucy, trying to control her situation.

"Ask your mother how she wants you to handle things," explained George's pastor. Asking for Elsa's advice would give her the autonomy she craves. "Tell her that you're all trying to make things work, and you sincerely want to keep her involved in the family dynamics."

After much prayer, George was able to talk to Elsa. He told her that belittling or criticizing Lucy is not allowed. They would work things out together, the three of them.

"Since I talked to my mother about how I felt squeezed between her and Lucy, things have improved," George told me. "I told Mom that she was an important part of our family, and we needed to get along. Sometimes she will join us in our prayer time together."

Blogger John Shore, who took care of his aging father, suggests offering parents options. "It's important for them to continue to feel as if they, and not you, are running their lives. Let them decide everything they can about their own care and situation," he says. Asking for your parent's advice (as George did) is another way to show your parent love and respect, and to affirm his or her value, Shore says.[1]

As you try to maintain your sanity as a caregiver, consider why your elderly parent is behaving a certain way. "Grief is a normal reaction to the loss of people, former lifestyles, relationships, health, vision, hearing, ability level, mobility, or independence," according to Zanda Hilger of the Area Agency on Aging. Yet if people have not coped well with loss and change in their younger years, aging can be especially difficult, Hilger adds. Some people may feel a sense of helplessness, or they may respond in any number of ways, such as being overly critical, rigid and stubborn, or depressed and anxious.[2]

"When people feel that they have little control over the present or have regrets about the past, they may react in anger," Hilger says. "They may lash out at family members—sometimes being most critical of those who are most supportive, since they know that these people will still love them in spite of their anger."[3]

Some elderly folks lose their ability to filter their speech and begin to make inappropriate comments in public. Have you heard these before? *That person is really fat. Young people these days don't know how to dress. Look at his pants sagging below his behind. Cashiers don't know how to count out change. They're dumb.* We need to be flexible and be able to shift boundary lines as we adjust to the new reality. When Mother speaks her mind, sometimes I bite my tongue and sometimes I make a comment, even if it's just to shush her. I find it's helpful to put a smile on my face and remind her of what she taught me: "If you can't say anything nice, don't say anything at all." This will diffuse the rebuke.

But when your loved one begins to verbally abuse you or others, it's time to step in. That's when the line must be drawn. To do this, first pray about how to approach your parent(s). Enlist the prayer support of a friend or pastor.

Second, speak humbly and with grace. "Pleasant words are a honeycomb, sweet to the soul and healing to the bones" (Proverbs 16:24). Replace "you" statements with "I" statements such as:

"I feel sad when you say those things to me."

"I won't be able to spend as much time with you if you continue to put me down."

"I love you, and I want to have a relationship with you, however . . ."

Third, be prepared for some pushback. If your relationship with your loved one has always been defined by abuse, don't expect it to change in an instant, or perhaps, ever.

It may be helpful to have a physician evaluate your loved one's condition. The mood and personalities of people with Alzheimer's can change. They can become confused, suspicious, depressed, fearful, or anxious. They may be easily upset at home, at work, with friends, or in places where they are out of their comfort zone. If the diagnosis is the beginning of Alzheimer's disease, you'll need to find resources to help deal with your loved one's gradual mental decline. The Alzheimer's Association (Alz.org) has a twenty-four-hour help line and local chapters to offer support for caregivers.

CHOOSE YOUR BATTLES

When my kids were teens, everything became a battleground: curfew, dating, clothes, hair, and driving privileges. As I sought help by reading parenting books, one piece of advice resonated with me: the need to pick your battles.

Now that I'm caring for my mother, I've returned to deciding which battles to fight. The other day we had the following conversation as Mom rode with me in my new car.

"Is this a Chevy?" she asked.

"Yes," I answered.

"You told me you bought a Buick."

"Why would I do that when I knew I bought a Chevy?"

"I don't know, but you told me it was a Buick. I even told Dodie you bought a Buick."

I stopped talking. Like the fruitlessness of arguing with a teenager, I decided my best course of action was to say nothing.

Other times, I must draw the line. Mom will pull me aside and ask me when I think Mike will have time to do a certain chore for her.

"I wouldn't ask him right now," I'll say. "He has a lot on his plate. Plus, I have some 'honey-do' things I need to have done."

I'll admit, the line in the sand seems faint—barely there—but it's the most I'm able to manage with my strong-willed mother. It's difficult to decide between choosing a battle and letting it pass.

What does Scripture advise? Colossians 4:6 says, "Let your conversation be always full of grace." In my experience with both my parents, that verse means sometimes I bite my lips to keep from responding to a barb. It means not being drawn into a negative conversation about a situation. Sometimes it means taking a deep breath before saying something I might regret. I have to ask myself if being right is truly important.

Grace Growers

1. Consider some of the parental boundaries you set with your children. Do you also need to set some boundaries with your aging loved ones for their good and yours?

2. Do you have a need to be "right" all the time? Think about how you can lay that aside and focus on your parents' needs.

3. Meditate on Proverbs 16:24 and Galatians 5:22–23: "But the fruit of the Spirit is love, joy, peace, patience, kindness, goodness, faithfulness, gentleness and self-control. Against

such things there is no law." Focus on exercising self-control. Think about how your words can be sweet to your loved ones' ears. Remember, "A gentle answer turns away wrath" (Proverbs 15:1).

10

NOURISHING BODY
AND SOUL

Then Jesus declared, "I am the bread of life.
He who comes to me will never go hungry, and
he who believes in me will never be thirsty."

JOHN 6:35

"What's for dinner this week?"

The question is the same every Sunday evening:
Mom wants to know what we've planned for the week's meals.
Before Dad died and Mom became incapacitated by constant
back pain, Mike and I used to eat out several times a week. Our
meals were often haphazard. When we did stay home, bowls of
cereal, peanut butter and jelly sandwiches, or scrambled eggs
would suffice. Since both of us love to experiment with recipes,
we'd revise our menu on the weekends when we had more time
to cook. That's when Mom and Dad often strolled to our house
to enjoy our culinary delights.

When Dad became wheelchair-bound, Mike would wheel

Dad to our house, with Mom clinging on his arm. After Dad died, Mom walked down to our house for dinner, often as many as three or four times a week.

"It's my only contact with the outside world," she told me.

"You're welcome to eat with us any time," I answered. I couldn't deny her human contact.

When she didn't have dinner with us, she'd eat like a teenager. Her favorites were pie with ice cream; a sweet roll; hamburger, fries, and a shake; or a McDonald's Frappé, all delivered to her by a well-meaning friend.

Slowly, Mom's physical health declined until she needed a walker to get around. She was terrified of falling, so Mike or I would walk her to our house. The three or four nights of dinner together per week became every night. I hated to see her eat junk food, and I felt responsible to ensure she ate a balanced meal at least once a day.

Many men and women don't like to cook for one person. When Mike is gone, I rarely fix a meal for myself. I understand why the elderly stop cooking.

"I've prepared dinner for the past sixty-plus years. I'm done," my mom announced.

I get it. I felt the same way after my kids moved out.

DIFFERENT NEEDS

Not only do seniors have different nutritional needs than younger adults, they also take more medication, have higher rates of chronic medical conditions—such as diabetes and heart disease—and are more likely to live alone; all of which contribute to the rising numbers of older Americans who are seriously impacted by a deficient diet.[1]

WATCH FOR DEPRESSION

Two years after Dad died, Mom sank into depression. Constant back pain kept her housebound and in bed most of the day. Even going to the doctor was an ordeal. Playing bridge was out of the question. I watched her appetite shrink. She'd eat a few bites of dinner, and then declare she was finished.

"I'm not hungry." She'd hunch over her plate, staring blankly at the food.

I tried coaxing her to eat, fixing some of her favorite things: lasagna, pork chops, macaroni and cheese. She wasn't even tempted when I made her all-time favorite, mashed potatoes and gravy. Every night was a repetition of the night before.

"I'm not hungry."

Mike tried bullying her. We coaxed, cajoled, and begged. After two weeks, Mom was too weak to come to the table. She talked about dying.

"How long does it take a person to starve to death?"

"What kind of a question is that?" Alarm bells rang in my head. Was Mom trying to die?

"I just want to know. Can you Google it?"

I gave her answers, but she persisted.

"What happens if a person stops eating and drinking? How long until they die?"

I called my brothers. "I think Mom is trying to kill herself."

My fears were realized when Mom asked, "Do you think I'll still go to heaven if I stop eating and drinking and die? Am I taking control away from God?"

Mike and I prayed about how to answer, and we talked with Mom at length about suicide and God's grace. We called a family meeting. Our daughter, Heather, flew down from Oregon, and my brothers came too.

As we gathered around Mom's bedside one Saturday morning, each of us told Mom how much we loved her. After recounting humorous and poignant memories of Mom and Dad, we told Mom that it was her decision about what to do. We spent a couple of hours together, closer as a family than we had been for a long time.

Later that evening, Mom and I reminisced about the day. She smiled for the first time in weeks.

"You know, I think I'll get up and have a little bite of applesauce," she said. She'd made the decision to live and to allow God to determine when her time on Earth was done. I cried with relief. She realized the truth of Psalm 139:16: "Your eyes saw my unformed body. All the days ordained for me were written in your book before one of them came to be." It took a lot of courage for Mom to make the choice. It wasn't an easy one. Each day, she wakes up with chronic pain. Every morning she wonders why she's still here. I encourage her to pray more, and she does. She has a prayer list of other women who need God's grace and His saving power.

About six million senior Americans (age sixty-five and older) suffer from depression. Of those, only 10 percent receive treatment for it.[2] The National Alliance on Mental Illness (NAMI) reports that there may be many reasons for this: Elderly people may think depression is a character flaw and are more likely to seek treatment for other physical ailments than for depression. In addition, depression in the elderly is also frequently confused with the effects of multiple illnesses. NAMI suggests a physical exam and a review of your elderly loved one's medications if you are concerned; in some cases a simple medication change can lessen the symptoms' intensity.[3] It's worth noting that in an elderly person, depression is sometimes characterized by memory problems, confusion, social withdrawal, loss of appetite, weight loss, vague complaints of pain, inability to sleep, irritability, delusions, and hallucinations.[4]

One way to guard against depression is by helping your parent remain socially engaged. Research suggests a strong connection between social interaction and health and well-being among older adults.[5] So as you care for your parent's nutrition, also make sure to consider his or her need for social contact. Nearly 11,000 senior centers in the United States offer a wide variety of activities, classes, and day trips. Living in a fifty-five-plus independent senior community also provides a built-in social club. Even a visit with a Meals on Wheels delivery person can brighten an elderly person's day. (Visit MealsonWheelsAmerica.org to find a service in your parent's area.)

FOOD AND FELLOWSHIP

As I consider other sons and daughters who are taking responsibility for their aging parents' health, I realize I'm part of a fellowship of caregivers bound not by DNA, but by God's grace. Darlene belongs to this fellowship.

When Darlene's eighty-six-year-old mom was finally able to go home from the hospital following surgery, Darlene and her sisters spent their days urging their mother to eat. Now Darlene continues to deliver dinner several nights a week, ensuring her mom will gain back her strength.

"I'm grateful to be able to show my mother how much I love her by fixing her favorite foods," Darlene said.

She told me it's only by God's grace that she continues to carry the responsibility for her mom, in addition to leading a women's Bible study, babysitting her grandson, and being active in her community.

So when it's 102 degrees at six o'clock at night and I'm dripping with sweat by the time I reach Mom's place with the evening meal, I remember that I'm not the only one responding to the responsibility of care. Some days I do it out of love. Some days I do it out of obligation. And every day I rely on God's grace to sustain me.

Sometimes Mom, Mike, and I sit around the dinner table and reminisce. We'll all start laughing so hard our eyes water. I cherish those times. It's in moments such as these that I realize I'm not just my mother's caregiver; I'm still her daughter, and I like the dual role.

Jesus spent the last night of His life having supper with His twelve closest friends; it was an intimate time of fellowship around the table. That same type of fellowship can be seen in churches when members provide meals for families when needed. Giving the physical nourishment of food often communicates love— which nourishes the soul.

When our son was undergoing chemo treatments at age seventeen, one friend said, "I will bring your family a meal every Tuesday until he's finished." Twenty years later, I still remember what a blessing it was to come home from the hospital and find dinner waiting on my back porch.

When Mike or I cook dinner for the three of us, we meet

more than just my mother's physical need. She looks forward to the social contact our nightly meal offers, even if we make a dish she doesn't like. It's important to view a shared meal with your parents as a social event. And while you're at your parents' home, check the pantry and fridge for expired food, encourage healthy snacking, and bring along foods packed with nutrients. Remember, too, that our loved ones' taste buds change as they age. This can be a result of hormonal changes, illness, or medications, so be sensitive to this as you prepare meals.

As you dine together, avoid difficult conversations. Instead, ask your parents about their favorite childhood memories. Talk about your day and ask for advice when appropriate. Make some new memories over lunch or dinner, and enjoy this season of providing physical, social, and spiritual nourishment for your parents.

Grace Growers

1. Take stock of your parent's social life and mental health status. Ask if he or she is feeling depressed.
2. How would you respond if your loved one talked about taking his or her life? Is there a pastor or spiritual counselor who can intervene? What do you think Psalm 139:16 means when it says, "All the days ordained for me were written in your book before one of them came to be"?
3. What nourishes you spiritually these days? A long quiet time with the Lord? Worship music? A walk in the woods? Make sure you are being fed so you can, in turn, feed your loved one with God's grace.
4. Meditate on John 6:35. Think about Jesus' words, "I am the bread of life." Fill your spirit with His life-giving bread.

NREALISTIC EXPECTATIONS

you answer yes to most of the following questions, you
ight have unrealistic expectations as a caregiver. If so, talk
a counselor or trusted friend and make adjustments for
e sake of your own mental health.

1. Do you feel that if you do not do it all, you do not care
   enough about your loved one?
2. Do you feel you have to do it all, do it well, and see
   to it that others are happy too?
3. Are you unable to set limits or boundaries in what
   you will or will not do?
4. Do you often go beyond the limits of your endurance?[3]

Otherwise, they remain unspoken and can cause much discord.
Before you begin a conversation with your loved one (assuming
your parent is cognitively able to have such a discussion), bring
it before God, asking the Lord to reveal issues in your heart and
in your parent's heart that may need His touch. And be sure to
examine what you expect of yourself or what others expect of you.
Are those expectations realistic?

When you are ready for a talk, begin by asking your parents
to pray with you. This sets the tone for God's grace to permeate
your spirit and your words. Make sure you let your loved ones
know that you want the best for them, and that this discussion will help meet that goal. Consider asking your parents these
questions to begin the conversation:

> Think about your normal day. What part do you expect
me to play in your day-to-day life? Do you assume I will

11

LETTING GO OF EXPECTATIONS

He has showed you, O man, what is good. And what
does the LORD require of you? To act justly and to
love mercy and to walk humbly with your God.

MICAH 6:8

As the youngest of three and the only girl, I admit I was
spoiled. My mother is an only child and her parents were
involved in our lives as far back as I can remember, so they were
always around to spoil me too. They even lived with us for a few
years when I was growing up.

After Mike and I married, my mom used to cook for us a
couple of times a week.

"You both work hard," my dad would say. "Let us take care
of you."

I liked being taken care of. It was easy to stay dependent on
my folks. I was grateful for the respite from having to plan and
cook meals, and I always expressed my thanks. Looking back,
I realize I expected to be taken care of. I don't remember ever

offering to help with grocery money. Not that my parents would have accepted it, but I viewed their service to me as my right.

Now the tables have turned. The expectations come from my mother, who is disappointed if we don't take dinner to her every night. I find myself becoming resentful. The more she expects, the more I resent.

Yet as caregivers, we can't expect our relationship with our parents to remain the same forever. Although we'll always be our parents' children, our new role carries us into uncharted waters.

When parents' expectations and goals clash with those of their adult child, emotions bubble to the surface. Unmet expectations on both sides can create resentment, and resentment grows into bitterness. For example, every time I visit Mom's house, she expects me to do a long list of tasks. The list is on a sticky note next to my dinner plate and usually looks like this:

> Pay these bills.
> Look something up on the web.
> Text your brother.

Mike's list is usually longer. She asks him to fix things—the lamp, the alarm, the phone. She tells him to empty the trash and bring in her mail because her chronic pain and macular degeneration do not allow her to do this.

The lists can overwhelm us and lead us to resentment. Unless we intervene, bitterness can wrap around our hearts. The Bible warns us about not letting the root of bitterness take hold, so I continually remind myself that I am a servant, first of Christ and then of my loved one. I can honor my mother by my willingness to

meet her expectations, knowing she's stuck in the
able to jump in the car and run to the store on a w
tion becomes a prison, and to her, small things be

"The bills have to be paid *right now*, or I'll get a
say. Or, "That lamp must be fixed *today*, or you'll
mind she's merely reminding us, but to Mike and
like nagging.

This is the place where laying down my life *ag*
wear on me. I'm exhausted from the effort. I want t
but my old nature rears its ugly head and says *no*.

Mike came up with a workable solution. Whe
yellow sticky next to his plate, he asks Mom when sl
each task done.

"Do you need it done tonight?" he'll ask. "Can I
row after work? How about if I take care of that thi

We've found a solution that everyone agrees wi
happy, Mike is happy.

"Most parents don't want to be a burden," says Ta
cofounder of Senior Care Solutions. "But there are u
pectations that kids will be there. 'When will you b
'How come you don't call more often?'"[1]

The fact that there are often basic differences with
about daily goals is common, says Allison Heid, proje
of the New Jersey Institute for Successful Aging. But th
ences can obviously be a barrier to providing support.

TALK ABOUT IT

As you care for your aging loved one, it's importan
about these different—and sometimes clashing—expe

help you in certain ways around the house, with errands, or financially? I want to make sure your needs are met, even if we may need to consider different ways to do this.

> How can you clearly let me know what your needs are? I won't be able to anticipate them. What system for communicating your needs will work well for you and for me?
> Will it be possible for me to meet all of your expectations while maintaining my physical, emotional, and spiritual health? Or will we need to consider some other options? What can we do to keep both of us healthy and happy?
> Have you thought of what will happen when you can't live by yourself any longer? What are your expectations for the future?

Bring everything into the light, leaving no opportunity for the devil to gain a foothold in your relationship with your aging loved one. Finally, *remember that your parents' or siblings' expectations are beyond your control. But you can control your expectations for yourself.*

Grace Growers

1. Write a list of what you expect of yourself as a caregiver. Then list your parents' and others' expectations of you. Ask yourself if you can humanly meet all of the expectations. Ask God to show you how to set realistic expectations for caregiving.
2. First Thessalonians 5:18 says to "give thanks in all circumstances, for this is God's will for you in Christ Jesus." Can

you obey this command, even if you don't feel able, and thank God for the privilege of caregiving?

3. Meditate on Micah 6:8: Consider God's expectations of you and how you've been given the opportunity to love mercy (some translations say "kindness") as you care for your aging loved one.

12
GUILTY OR NOT GUILTY?

Guilt isn't always a rational thing. Guilt is a weight
that will crush you, whether you deserve it or not.

MAUREEN JOHNSON, AUTHOR

M om would be shocked to hear I feel guilty when she asks
me certain questions.

"You're not bringing me dinner tomorrow night?"

"I have to eat alone? Again?"

"When will you be home?"

"Can you make time in your busy schedule to do something
for me?"

When I hear questions like these, sometimes I want to react
in a way that isn't Christlike. But I'm not the only one who feels
guilty. Sometimes Mom expresses *her* guilt over relying on Mike
and me so much.

"You should have more of a life," she once told me when I
was spending time with her during a midweek work holiday. "I
feel bad you have to bring me dinner every night. I know it's hard
on you."

It would have been disingenuous of me to deny that sometimes I felt burdened by having to march down to her house every evening, cooking pots in hand, juggling keys, serving dishes, and other miscellaneous stuff. I kept silent, hoping she'd do more than express her feelings. I was hoping those guilt-laden sentences of hers would disappear.

The next night, I decided to go to the gym after work. Mike delivered dinner to Mom's and they ate without me. The following night I had a meeting. For three nights in a row, I didn't make the thousand-foot journey to Mom's for the nightly dinner ritual.

The next evening I walked in and greeted Mom with a cheery, "Howdy!"

"Oh, do you still live here?" she asked.

Snarky? Oh, yes. Guilt producing? Yes, again.

This is her way of saying, "I missed you."

I bit my tongue.

GUILT TRIP

Mike and I talked about our options regarding the commitment to provide meals for Mom. We'd put ourselves into a frustrating situation, by our own choice. We'd offered to take dinner to my mother every night, not realizing the long-term impact on our physical and emotional health. Since then, we've come to an agreement and set some boundaries, but at that time we couldn't see clearly.

Experts all agree that taking care of yourself and your needs is vital to maintaining your ability to help your loved one. Yet sometimes I feel guilty for wanting to exercise after work, which means I'll miss dinner with Mike and my mom. When I talk with other caregivers about these feelings, we all agree that battling guilt is a normal part of the caregiving season.

My friend Charles shared with me that his mom, who's been living with him and his wife for seven years, admitted she needed care beyond what Charles and Verna could provide. They began the process of applying for a state-funded program to help pay for an assisted-living home. I asked if he'd be relieved when a place became available.

He said no. He still feels guilty on so many different levels: that he can no longer provide the care for his mom; that he and his wife can't afford to pay for a nice place with a single-occupancy apartment in an upscale facility; that his mom currently pays a small amount toward the rent on the home; that he is her sole caregiver, and as such, is paid a stipend by the county government.

My friend John has a father suffering from dementia. By default, John has to make the decision about what to do with his dad. His brother is either unwilling or incapable of determining what to do. John and his wife have discussed all the options: full-time, in-home care; an assisted-living facility; moving in with his father; or adult day care. Each option carries its own weight of guilt. His dad doesn't make it any easier. On his bad days, he accuses John of stealing his mail, hiding his car keys, and moving things around. When I greet John at church, I see the stress in his eyes.

Peter Rosenberger, in his book, *Hope for the Caregiver*, says it best: "The guilt of making unilateral decisions, particularly for spouses and children caring for elderly parents, can be crushing. We're mobile, they're not. They're in pain, we're not. They cling—we feel suffocated."[1]

Our normal exit route from our condo took us right by the folks' house. Many times Mom would call and ask where we were going. Sometimes Mike and I slipped out in the other direction, guiltily sliding down in our seats in case Mom happened to glance out the kitchen window instead. Then a lively discussion would ensue.

"Do you think we should have asked your folks to go out to dinner with us?" Mike would ask.

> Change "guilt" to "regret." Guilt is you did something wrong, regret is that you are in a difficult situation and sometimes you have to make difficult decisions, but they are not wrong.
>
> **FAMILY CAREGIVER ALLIANCE**

"No," I'd respond. "We need time alone."

"You're right. It'll be fine."

Then my guilty feelings would kick in.

"Maybe we should have. They'd probably love to get out of the house."

"Yeah," Mike would agree.

Some typical guilty thoughts would be: *My parents have done so much for me over the years, how can I not help them? I should take them with me every time I go out. I should involve them more in my life. I should do more because I'm the only daughter and because I live the closest. I should, I should, I should.* There's no inoculation against guilt; rather, the question is how I deal with it. This is my ongoing balancing act: If I do everything for my parents, I slip into martyrdom. If I do too little, I've retreated into selfishness.

Caregiving can be especially guilt producing when the relationship between parent and adult child hasn't been healthy. "Relationship baggage typically doesn't get better with caregiving," says Taryn Benson, cofounder of Senior Care Solutions. "Instead of a delight or desire to care for their parent, it becomes a duty. . . . Usually adult children who struggle with this dynamic need to engage other siblings, family, or friends, or seek professional assistance."[2]

NO ONE'S PERFECT

The Family Caregiver Alliance reminds us in "A Guide to Taking Care of Yourself," "As there is no 'perfect parent,' there is no such thing as a 'perfect' caregiver. And you are not selfish to sometimes think about yourself and your needs and feelings."[3]

Keep in mind that the enemy of our souls would love to deceive us by letting us think we're "bad" because we need time for ourselves. So "be self-controlled and alert," as it says in 1 Peter 5:8. When you start taking on blame and guilt, remind yourself of all the good things you do, such as:

> *I take my dad to the Sunday swap meet once a month, and let him walk around by himself and chat with his buddies.*
> *I run errands for my mom, even though it's my day off.*
> *I provide meals for my mom five days a week.*

If you have misguided guilt feelings about caring for your elderly loved one, a Christian counselor or clergyperson can help. What

MISGUIDED GUILT

It is useful to distinguish between misguided guilt and true guilt. Suppose you are doing everything possible for your aging loved one, yet you feel it is not nearly good enough or often enough. . . . Admit that you are doing your best and learning to do better. Give yourself credit for what you are able to do, knowing your needs are important.

If you feel guilty about circumstances beyond your control, you may be imposing guilt on yourself. . . . The remedy? Start by refusing to criticize yourself or dwell on your inadequacies. Dwell instead on what you can do, relying on the faithfulness and goodness of the God who created and redeemed you.[4]

you feel is common when we become overwhelmed. You may be able to find a caregiver support group in your area. AgingCare.com has a discussion forum on all topics related to caregiving. There's also a link to all the agencies available in each state for support.

As I learn to turn my feelings over to the Lord, He is faithful to reward me in many ways. Sometimes it's an unexpected gift from Mom—flowers from her camellia bush, or some homemade muffins. Other times He shows me how blessed I am to still have my mother to turn to, a mother who loves me and celebrates with me. Many women mourn the loss of their mothers and their special shared relationship. Just a few days ago, my mother called me while I was on my way to speak to a group of women. She knows I get nervous before speaking in public.

"You'll do great," she encouraged me. "You're a good speaker. Call me when you're done and let me know how you did."

I called her on my way home to let her know my talk went well.

"I knew you'd be fine," she said. My heart warmed to her love. How blessed I am to still have her with me. At that moment, guilt had no place in my heart.

Grace Growers

1. As you care for your parent, where are the places guilt creeps in to bind you? Is it misguided guilt or true guilt? Make a list of the care that you do provide, of the things you "do right."

2. Was your relationship with your loved one healthy in your growing-up years? If not, can you ask the Lord to redeem the relationship?

3. Meditate on Romans 8:1. Give thanks to God for the release from condemnation and guilt. Think about the many times King David confessed his true guilt to the Lord, and how God continually forgave him.

13

HEART CARE

Mike called me one evening while I was out of town, baby-sitting my three grandchildren so my daughter and son-in-law could attend a missions conference.

"Don't freak out," he said. When someone begins a conversation with *Don't freak out*, the natural thing to do is just that. I braced myself for what was coming.

"Mom had a couple of little heart attacks and she's on her way to the hospital."

I didn't freak out. What could I do? I was six hundred miles away, carrying the responsibility for three little kids. I knew in my heart Mom would be okay. This time.

But my heart also knows Mom won't live forever. It has been five years since my dad passed, and she's ready to go. I'm preparing myself for that day when Mom leaves to be with her Savior.

She's scared, so we talk a lot about heaven and eternal life. She's more afraid of the actual process of dying than she is of death.

Part of my caregiving is tending to my Mom's heart—her emotional and spiritual needs—so I continually reassure Mom that her life is in God's hands. He's the only one who knows the number of her days. He's the giver and taker of life. She's terrified she'll have a stroke and end up like so many of her friends who have already died—helpless, stuck in limbo between this world and the next. Each time she brings it up, I remind her I'll always be there for her, to care, visit, and do what's necessary.

"Remember when you visited Nini [my grandmother] at Manor Care every single day?" I tell her, "I'll do the same for you."

I hold her heart gently, the one who carried me for nine months, who cared for me and gave me more than things. My mom still worries about me, even though I'm heading into my sixth decade. If I'm not feeling well, she thaws homemade applesauce for me. When someone at work gives me a hard time, she's vocal in my defense. Both she and my dad delighted in my successes through my growing-up years, and Mom continues to delight in my achievements.

WHEN HEARTS ARE APART

Not everyone is blessed in this way. My mother's heart attacks were physical, yet some caregivers have experienced emotional heart attacks: assaults that have come from their own parents. Caregiving is even more of a challenge when the relationship with one or both of our parents is difficult.

Stephon and his wife cared for his mom in their home before

she passed away. Their relationship had always been strained. His mother belittled him until the day she died. He wishes they could have reconciled, or at least been at peace with each other. Two years later, he still struggles to forgive, his heart hardened by years of verbal abuse.

Danicka refuses to visit her dying mother because of the cutting remarks she's endured her entire life. When Danicka and her sister moved their mom into a convalescent hospital, their mother continued to chip away at Danicka's self-image. The comments were so ugly that Danicka had to fly home early to escape her mother's constant abuse. She's working through the forgiveness process with God's help. We've talked about guarding her heart so it won't become hardened.

Focus on the Family president Jim Daly, who himself grew up in a dysfunctional family, offers this advice:

> As hard as it may seem, we believe it's important to reach
> out to your parents . . . and to forgive them. Even when
> they're not seeking that forgiveness, we can choose to
> give respect and care to our elders. True honor is placing
> the highest value on our loved ones whether they deserve
> it or not.
>
> You can't change the painful events of your childhood
> or alter your parents' choices. But you can refuse to give
> their problems power over you. . . . Caring for your
> parents doesn't necessarily mean agreeing with everything
> they say, or giving in to their every demand. It simply
> means doing what you can within a realistic framework
> to live at peace with your aging parents. It means making

wise choices that will keep your conscience clear. When they're gone, you don't want to look back on this time and regret not reaching out to them.[1]

Through the Holy Spirit's power, we can find strength to forgive even those who do not forgive us and those who refuse to apologize, notes Nancy Parker Brummett in her book *Take My Hand Again: A Faith-Based Guide for Helping Aging Parents.* She goes on to say,

> Remember . . . to pray together for forgiveness for the two of you—for those shortcomings and sins you are aware of and any that have conveniently escaped your attention. However, . . . this is probably not the time to go into the specifics of every offense. . . .
>
> It may be more productive to say something like, "I know we haven't always been all we could have been to one another, but I want you to know I forgive you for that, and I hope you can forgive me." Blanket forgiveness is better than no forgiveness at all.[2]

Some caregivers find themselves wishing for their mother's or father's death. Then comes the guilt for feeling that way.

"If a parent's attitude and behavior don't improve, the child wants an end to the suffering. That can only come when the parent dies," writes Mark Goulston in *Psychology Today.*[3]

It's normal to want the suffering to end. Speak with a counselor, pastor, or trusted adviser if feelings of wanting your parent to die become an obsession. Ask for help. Pray for God's guidance, and remember that these feelings are normal. Frustration and anger are a part of caring for an elderly loved one, and even more so when that loved one is difficult.

For caregiver Mary Alexander, trusting God was the key to surving the stress of her role:

> There is no easy road, no easy way, no easy answer.
> One good day can be followed by an avalanche of bad
> days. And, to be honest, at times my faith wavered.
> The days when I lacked belief in God were the darkest.
> Without the belief that there is a presence greater than
> myself to help me through the daily trials, life just
> didn't make sense. But I learned to choose not to be
> angry and just trust that God was there for me and
> my family. I learned that closing my heart is never the
> answer. Keeping an open heart to God in the face of
> adversity is the key that unlocks the power of selfless
> service to others.[4]

SOFT HEARTS

Martha Stettinius says she was a "reluctant" caregiver of her mother, a recovering alcoholic. Even though her mom had been sober for thirty-five years, Martha still remembered being a young teen cooking dinner while her mom was passed out on her bed.

Yet as Stettinius spent more time caring for her mother, her reluctance melted away.

> I learned that caring for my mother was about more
> than doing things for her—it was also about just

"being" with her. Even when she lost her language
we could still communicate through touch, our facial
expressions, and body language. Even if she could no
longer say my name, I could see in her eyes how much
she loved me.

I cared for Mom for eight years, and I'm so very
grateful that we had that time together. Our caregiving
journey healed what was left of the conflicts between us.[5]

Caregiving enlarges our hearts if we let God into the process.
When we bring our hearts to the Lord, His love can compel us
to show grace in this season and come to terms with our parents
before they leave this life. The more I open up my heart when
caring for my parent, the bigger it grows. I've learned to let go of
many of the little things that used to annoy me. I'm more open
to giving my mother a hug when we say good-bye. I don't resent
calling her when I return home after being out at night to reassure her I'm home safe.

To keep my heart open, I must continually guard it in the
midst of my mom's sometimes overwhelming needs. Sometimes
guarding my heart is as easy as remembering something special about our relationship. Other times it takes lots of prayer.
When I'm finished dumping all my frustration on God, He
never answers, "You shouldn't feel that way, Jane. Shame on you."
Instead, He reminds me of His grace. Jesus must have been frustrated over the crowds' demands to show them a miracle. Yet He
responded with grace and love. He is my example, and I am His
hands and feet on earth—not just to my aging loved one, but
also to the world.

Grace Growers

1. Have you wished your loved one would die? Talk to the Lord about your feelings as the psalmist does in Psalm 25:17: "The troubles of my heart have multiplied; free me from my anguish." Then take any thought of death captive, as instructed in 2 Corinthians 10:5: "We demolish arguments and every pretension that sets itself up against the knowledge of God, and we take captive every thought to make it obedient to Christ."

2. In what way does your heart need to be enlarged as you care for your aging loved one? Try praying Psalm 26:2: "Test me, O LORD, and try me, examine my heart and my mind." Ask the Lord to soften your heart where needed and to fill it with love that will overflow to your parents.

3. Meditate on Psalm 73:26: "My flesh and my heart may fail, but God is the strength of my heart and my portion forever." What a relief to know that God is our strength, whether we are the caregiver or an elderly person with an aging body! Share this verse with your loved one if you can. Ask God to strengthen your heart today.

14

MONEY TALKS

"The silver is mine and the gold is mine,"
declares the LORD Almighty.

HAGGAI 2:8

Talking to Mom and Dad about their money doesn't usually make people's "top ten list" of fun things to do. It wasn't on my list either, but I had to do it anyway.

Last year, my mother became ill with a bacterial infection, resulting in a five-day hospital stay and recovery at a convalescent hospital. Mike and I weren't sure she'd be able to come home, since the infection left her weak and barely able to keep food down. Since it didn't look like she'd be released from the convalescent hospital any time soon, I signed up for online banking on her account and started paying her bills.

When Mom finally returned to her home and routine after four weeks, the first thing she did was to call the bank and then give me the third degree.

"What's going on with my account?" Mom demanded. "This isn't right! Have you been in my account?"

Mom's outrage shot from her eyes, turning her face red.

Stunned into silence, I could only gape at her.

She eventually calmed down when I explained I had paid her bills and transferred money from checking to savings.

Many people I've talked to tell the same kind of stories. As their parents age, money may become an issue. If they are fearful of not having enough to live on until they die, some elders may be overly protective of their assets. Seniors who have lived through the Depression are especially careful.

My mom clearly remembers the struggles her family faced during those years. She lived with her parents, her aunt and uncle, and another couple in a two-bedroom apartment. Seven people living in a two-bedroom apartment requires a lot of grace. My grandpa searched for any kind of day labor he could find, often returning home with only a few cents. My grandma worked in a department store, taking in ironing and mending on the side.

The struggles my mom faced had such an impact on her that she still refuses to throw away anything that might possibly, even remotely, be used again. Mike and I often remark that her careful budgeting of every penny borders on obsession.

Parents can have deep issues with money based on societal mores and the need to keep up appearances. For some, talking about money directly is just not done. It's embarrassing, improper, scary, and just generally uncomfortable. For many, having their kids know everything about their finances is extra humbling.

Getting involved in our parents' finances intrudes upon three key aspects of our relationship with our parents, according to Sharon Burns and Raymond Forgue. "One, both parents and children value their ability to handle their own affairs. Two, they guard their privacy. Three, they try to avoid conflict." Burns and Forgue go on to say that children who once told their parents, "I can take care of myself," are now hearing their parents tell them the same thing.[1]

Some people's parents accuse them of stealing money even though they are doing their best to care for their folks' finances. My friend David is a CPA, and so was his father, Abe. Once a week, Abe shows up at David's office with a pile of bills and his checkbook. He tosses them onto his son's desk saying, "Pay these."

Because Abe is in the early stages of dementia, David knows that no matter what he does, Abe will criticize. David pays the bills, returns everything to Abe, and then is subjected to bitter accusations of misusing his dad's funds. No matter how many times David reviews the finances, Abe is sure David is stealing from him. This continues until the following week, when the scenario starts over.

As Christians, we endeavor to follow the Lord's command to "Honor your father and your mother," even when we're accused of mishandling our parents' finances. In 1 Corinthians 13:5 we read, "[Love] is not rude, it is not self-seeking, it is not easily angered, it keeps no record of wrongs." Living out this verse, even while our parents are suspicious of us, means keeping an attitude of forgiveness. For me, it's a constant, moment-by-moment walk to keep resentment from hindering my walk before the Lord.

BEWARE OF SCAMS

Caregivers must also be vigilant about scams targeting the elderly. My mother, like many other elderly people, could easily fall prey to rip-offs.

My mom's phone rang one fall morning.

"Grandma?" asked the male voice on the other end.

"Mark?" Mom asked. Since the death of our son, Bobby, the only man to call her Grandma is Bobby's best friend, Mark.

"Yeah. I'm in trouble."

"What's wrong?"

The young man explained that he'd been in a traffic accident and was in jail. He needed to have money wired to him via Western Union.

"What about your folks?" Mom asked.

"Oh, no, I can't ask them right now. They'd be really upset."

My mom explained that she'd need to get a ride to the nearest Western Union, since she no longer drove.

Thankfully she called me immediately. I told her that Mark would never ask her to wire money, regardless of the reason. He'd ask his parents before anyone else. I reminded her that scam artists prey on vulnerable seniors like her.

Thirty minutes later, the bold con artist called back.

"Have you wired the money yet, Grandma?" he asked.

"Sorry, no," Mom answered. "You're going to have to stay in jail."

The caller cursed, then hung up.

Seniors are exploited financially at an extremely high rate, with one in twenty older adults indicating some form of perceived financial mistreatment in the recent past. Yet studies show that "only one in forty-four cases of financial abuse is ever reported."[2]

Monica Daggs, vice president for trading and operations at CUSO Financial Services in San Diego, California, says a common fraud is "an e-mail scheme where a criminal will get access to a client's email account, then send an email to the financial advisor, posing as the client and saying there's an urgent need for funds—say a family crisis."[3]

It's even more shocking to discover that 90 percent of senior financial abuse is at the hands of family members or trusted others.[4] The elderly are also financially exploited by caregivers, scam artists, financial advisers, home repair contractors, fiduciaries (such as agents under power of attorney and guardians), and others.[5]

I read a story about a son who took advantage of his mother's trust. He conspired with the family's "trusted" financial adviser to move his mother's investments, and then took out a loan against them. The transaction garnered a huge commission for the broker and provided funds the son needed to start a business. However, the son did not intend to pay back the loan.

If your parents are still living independently, make sure you review common scams with them. The National Adult Protective Services Association warns against the following signs of possible financial exploitation:

> Termination of vital utilities such as telephone, water, electricity/gas, or garbage
> Unpaid bills and liabilities despite adequate income
> Oversight of finances surrendered to others without explanation or consent
> Transferring assets to new "friends" assisting with finances
> Checks written to "Cash"
> Does not understand his/her current finances, offers improbable explanations
> Unexplained disappearance of cash, valuable objects, financial statements

> Unexplained or unauthorized changes to wills or other estate documents
> Giving away money or spending [extravagantly]
> Appearance of property liens or foreclosure notices[6]

HAVING THE TALK

I've struggled to talk with my mom about her finances. She is secretive about her stash. At the beginning of every month, she hands me a large check to cash for her. An attached sticky note lists the desired number and denomination of the bills. What cash isn't used goes into a hiding place. *For what?* I want to ask. *What are you saving for, since you can't go anywhere to spend money?* If pressed, she closes up like a vacation home in the winter. *Security*, I think. *It's a symbol of security.*

She worries daily she won't have enough money to keep her

COMMON SCAMS BY STRANGERS
> Lottery and sweepstakes scams: "You've already won! Just send $2,500 to cover your taxes."
> Home repair/traveling con men: "We're in your area and can coat your driveway/roof really cheaply."
> Grandparent scam: You're called and told your grandson is in jail and needs you to send money immediately.
> Charity scams: falsely soliciting funds for good causes; very common after disasters.
> "I'm from the utility company; I need you to come outside with me for a minute" (while accomplice steals valuables).
> Telemarketing scams and accompanying threats
> Money sent via telegraphs to people claiming lottery winnings[7]

---

until she dies. She worries she won't have anything to leave us kids, as if we're expecting some huge inheritance. I can understand why she'd want to be protective, hovering over her dwindling retirement money.

Talking about money can also involve shame. Our elders may feel shame that they didn't prepare enough for retirement. They may also fear becoming dependent on their children for support as they age or dread having to rely on government assistance for care. The average cost of a nursing home is almost $7,000 per month for a private room and around $6,500 for semi-private. Most seniors haven't saved their entire lives to spend their money on end-of-life care.

Financial guru Dave Ramsey says the subject of finances "will always be touchy and emotional, so expect that when you talk about them. Remember to speak adult-to-adult with parents about money and financial matters. It will make things easier for both of you."[8]

Unlike anything else, it seems money issues dig deep into our motives. Frank conversations about finances reveal our basic fears and temptations, as well as the lies we tell ourselves. I have friends whose families have split apart because of money. Both before the parents' passing, and after, seeming inequalities between family members can fester and boil. Consider the danger of waiting too long to talk about money when it comes to matters of inheritance.

"The lack of a will increases the likelihood of family battles and hard feelings," say Burns and Forgue. "And family members are left to second-guess what the deceased person's true wishes really were."[9]

I've talked with my mother about where she wants her money

to go after she passes. She said she wants Mike and me to inherit the bulk of it, since we've been the primary caregivers. At first, I thought, *Good, we should get more. I've been the dutiful daughter. Mike has been more than a son-in-law.* This attitude followed me for several days, until the Holy Spirit pricked my heart. He reminded me of 1 Corinthians 13, about love not keeping a record of wrong. How could I think I deserve more than my brothers do?

Read Romans 12:3 for a reminder of the attitude Christ wants us to have: "For by the grace given me I say to every one of you: Do not think of yourself more highly than you ought, but rather think of yourself with sober judgment, in accordance with the measure of faith God has given you."

If we're not careful, money can become a symbol of love, conjuring up strong emotions. When I talked with my mother about how she wanted her money divided, she reminded me that it was her money to do with what she wanted. Her decisions have nothing to do with how much she loves me, or how much she loves my brothers. I also have to remember that while she's alive, she makes the decisions for how she spends her money. After she's gone, the only change is who writes the checks according to my mother's wishes.

To separate yourself from any claim on your parents' money, it helps to remember that God is your provider, not your parents. Pastor Rick Warren expands on the truth of Philippians 4:19: God will meet your financial needs (not wants) if you ask for His help, learn to be content, practice giving in faith, maintain financial integrity, and trust Him with your life—completely.[10] If your parents are Christians, reminding them of this verse could also help allay fears.

The Bible talks about money 121 times in 111 verses. It's an important subject for God's people. "Keep your lives free from the love of money and be content with what you have, because God has said, 'Never will I leave you; never will I forsake you'" (Hebrews 13:5). What a wonderful reminder of how God wants us to view our finances and those of our parents.

> **And my God will meet all your needs according to his glorious riches in Christ Jesus.**
>
> **PHILIPPIANS 4:19**

Sometimes a third party, such as a financial planner or counselor, is necessary to act as an intermediary when having a conversation with aging loved ones. DaveRamsey.com has a wealth of information regarding finances. You can also check the Christian Financial Planner Directory (ChristianPF.com) to find a financial planner in your area.

Grace Growers

1. Make a list of money issues you're facing as you care for your parents. Pray for God's guidance and viewpoint on each issue.
2. Are you serving your loved one with no thought of financial gain? Meditate on Matthew 6:24: "No one can serve two masters. Either he will hate the one and love the other, or he will be devoted to the one and despise the other. You cannot serve both God and Money."
3. Read Luke 12:24, Psalm 34:10, and Matthew 6:31–32. Next, list the ways God has provided for you in the past. Finally, ask God to help you release any claims to your parents' money.

15

GIVE ME A BREAK

Come to me, all you who are weary and burdened,
and I will give you rest.

MATTHEW 11:28

"Mom, Mike and I are going on vacation next month." I spoke the words softly, hoping to lessen the impact.

Mom's head shot up. Raw panic filled her eyes.

"How long will you be gone?" she asked. Her voice trembled, and I wasn't sure if the shakiness was because of age or fear.

I decided to get the news over with quickly, telling myself it would be like yanking off a bandage—painful but necessary.

"A week."

"A week?" Mom's voice rose.

This is a typical scenario every time I want to leave town for more than a day.

Questions bounce around in Mom's mind. *Who will take care of me? What if I fall? What will I eat? I'll be lonely.* Mom's comfort is in knowing we're just down the street. She becomes unsettled when we're not close by and worries about every little thing that could go wrong.

"Mom, you'll be fine," Mike says. "You have a son a few minutes away, remember?"

Mom purses her lips. Mike and I know what she's thinking. *That's not an option.* But we know it is. My brother will come through in an emergency.

Even though my brother is nearby, I'm the one who feels the pull of Mom's apron strings tightening around me. But I want to get away. I *need* to get away—and so do you.

Short breaks and longer respites are vital for caregivers' health. Consider the health risks associated with long-term caregiving:

> Eighty percent of caregivers say they feel a great deal of stress.
> Fifty percent have clinically significant depression.
> Anxiety is higher in caregivers than among non-caregivers.
> Caregivers have more physical health problems.
> Caregivers have poorer immune system function and slower healing of wounds.
> Caregivers experience more colds and other viral illnesses.[1]

I'll be the first to admit that taking a break isn't easy. When I prepare for a vacation, I need a spreadsheet to put everything together for my mother's care. I prevail upon friends to provide meals. Neighbors are asked to stop in and visit. Any doctors' appointments have to be orchestrated with someone who can drive Mom to the clinic. I fill in every blank to be sure I've covered everything. The apron strings tighten around my chest, threatening to choke me.

Most of the people I know who care for their parents, whether hands-on or not, say they face the same struggle. Finding someone to watch Mom or Dad so caregivers can get away is "Mission Impossible." Friends are busy, and relatives have something else to do. I hear their heart-cry: *I just need a day or two away!*

My friend called me the other day. "I've had it," Jean said. "My mother-in-law is driving me crazy. She won't do anything I say. She ignores the healthy food I make for her and goes for the junk food instead. She refuses to take a shower. I don't know what to do anymore."

Jean's mother-in-law, Marge, lives with Jean and her husband, Eric. Even though Eric's brother and his wife live three minutes away, their mother's care defaulted to Jean.

"I'm going to sit the boys down this weekend and let them know I'm done. They're going to have to figure it out themselves. Then I'm taking a spa day."

This is the burden of many caregivers. Jean holds down a demanding, full-time job, volunteers to organize charity fundraisers, and offers her expertise to business development associations. Every morning she heads to the gym for a workout and then returns home to prepare breakfast for her mother-in-law, who is on a restricted diet because of diabetes and circulatory problems. She also prepares Marge's healthy lunch so the part-time caregiver can warm it in the microwave. When Jean arrives home from work, she fixes dinner for Eric, Marge, and their college-age son. She's happy to do it, but often finds herself tired and cranky.

She's not the only woman who occasionally feels this way, mainly because there are so many others in the same situation: an estimated 66 percent of caregivers are women.[2] The average caregiver is a forty-nine-year-old woman who is married and employed.[3] Not only that, female caregivers may spend as much as 50 percent more time providing care than male caregivers.[4]

Why do women generally tend to be the kin keepers, the ones who nurture and provide care? It might be due in part to the chemical and structural differences between male and female brains. Females process more oxytocin (a bonding relationship chemical) than males. Females also often have a higher density of neural connections into the hippocampus, the memory center of the brain, which is larger in women. As a result, women tend to absorb more emotive information than males, as well as more information to and from all five senses.[5]

Not only that, women tend to have verbal centers on both sides of the brain, while males tend to have verbal centers on only the left hemisphere. Because of this, females tend to use more words when discussing an incident, story, person, object, feeling, or place. Males also have less connectivity between their word centers and their memories or feelings.[6]

"When it comes to discussing feelings and emotions and senses together, girls tend to have an advantage," writes Gregory L. Jantz, PhD, in *Psychology Today*.[7]

We don't wake up one day and become our parents' keepers. We gradually slide into the role, unaided for the most part by our male siblings.

To be fair, some wonderful sons do tenderly care for their parents, and some men provide better care for their parents than their sisters. I'll freely admit that my husband is kinder, gentler, and more patient with my mom (and dad when he was living) than I am.

GIVE YOURSELF GRACE

Among women tending to their parents or in-laws, burnout is common. The responsibility rests heavily on our shoulders. We feel the weight of every pain and sickness—every fall, blood pressure crash, blood pressure spike, heart palpitation, urinary tract infection, and every case of pneumonia. We're on call for every need: We fill prescriptions; we run to urgent care and the emergency room; we dash to the store to buy Tylenol. We respond to every desire, whether our loved one is craving frozen yogurt or forgot to buy something at the store. The list is as endless as the ocean crashing into the shore. We're the "need-meeters," and we anticipate needs even before they're expressed.

I wonder if Mom needs something. I should call Mom before I go. Should I pick something up while I'm out?

Women tend to focus outwardly on others' needs—especially those of our husbands, children, and our parents. When we don't take time to keep ourselves healthy, our immune systems become weak and we become ill. Men can also fall into a work-at-all-costs mode, doing more and more until a major health crisis hits.

As Christians, we tend to take very seriously the words of Philippians 2:3–4: "Do nothing out of selfish ambition or vain conceit, but in humility consider others better than yourselves. Each of you should look not only to your own interests, but also to the interests of others." A very wise pastor preached on this passage several years ago, explaining that it's okay to consider your own needs as long as you also help others in their need. If you're a woman, take a hard look at your schedule. Don't neglect your own health and spiritual well-being by being "the good child." My doctor warned me to guard my health like the treasure it is—he's seen too many women caregivers burn out and become sick themselves.

> **It is so important as a caregiver not to become so enmeshed in the role that you lose yourself. It's neither good for you nor your loved one.**
> **DANA REEVE**
> Author of *Care Packages: Letters to Christopher Reeve from Strangers and Other Friends*

As we offer God's grace to our elderly loved ones, we must also remember to give grace to ourselves. This also applies to the many baby boomers who feel the inescapable pull of the apron strings from across the country. Marion's mother lives in an assisted-living facility. Her health has declined steadily over the past several months. Marion is being forced to make a decision: transfer her mom to a place that offers more hands-on care, or move her mother in with her. The decision would be easier if Marion's mother didn't live four hundred miles away.

Nate's parents lived in a retirement community in another state. After his mother died, Nate's dad floundered. Nate urged his dad to move to California so he'd be nearer. Nate was able to move his father into a retirement community a few miles from his home. For some, however, a move isn't possible.

Patty's mother lives across the country. Patty's sister provides emotional support for their mother, who lives in a convalescent hospital. Patty spends a lot of money flying back and forth to help her sister every time her mom has a medical emergency. Lately, it seems that event occurs monthly.

ASK FOR HELP

Whether parents are hundreds of miles away or right next door, we all need to ask for God's grace. We need grace to deal with the guilt of not always being there and grace to give ourselves permission for self-care. We also need to employ every community resource, neighbor, friend, family member, and technological tool available so we can care for our parents and ourselves.

If you are reluctant to seek help, ask yourself why this is. God wants to care for you as well as your elderly loved one. He reminds of us this in Luke 12:6–7: "Are not five sparrows sold for two pennies? Yet not one of them is forgotten by God. Indeed, the very hairs of your head are all numbered. Don't be afraid; you are worth more than many sparrows."

To make it easier to ask for assistance, the Family Caregiver Alliance suggests being prepared with a mental task list. Then when someone asks how he or she can help you, you'll have something concrete to suggest. "For example, someone could take the person you care for on a fifteen-minute walk a couple of times a week. Your neighbor could pick up a few things for you at the grocery store. A relative could fill out some insurance papers. When you break down the jobs into very simple tasks, it is easier for people to help."[8]

Having a backup plan for when Mike and I are gone helps

alleviate some of my mom's angst. We've asked a few neighbors and friends for their contact information, and I've made a list of people my mother can call in case something happens. We live in a townhome complex, so I make sure she knows whom to call if she has a plumbing or electrical problem. I've also found it helps ease my mother's mind if I take the time to call her once a day while I'm away. Whether I'm on an overnight trip with friends or on a week-long visit to my grandchildren, merely hearing my voice every day seems to be enough to allay her fears.

One of my favorite Bible verses is 1 Corinthians 2:7: "No, we speak of God's secret wisdom, a wisdom that has been hidden and that God destined for our glory before time began." At our time of greatest need, God has already given us the wisdom to deal with the situations we face. We simply need to call upon it. Ask God to show you if you are nearing burnout and how to handle it if you are.

The symptoms of caregiver burnout are similar to the symptoms of stress and depression. They include emotional and physical exhaustion, irritability, changes in sleep patterns, getting sick more often, feeling helpless or hopeless, wanting to hurt the one you're caring for, and changes in appetite, weight, or both.

"Honestly, we have to get some space. . . . We caregivers need to get away on a regular basis," says Peter Rosenberger in *Hope for the Caregiver*.[9] "Taking some time off for yourself is not a sign of weakness and will help you more than you may realize."[10]

The caregivers I know say that taking time away is the most important thing they do for themselves. Whether that means a day of shopping with friends, time on the golf course, or a weekend getaway, they return refreshed and ready to shoulder the responsibility once again.

"Everybody talks about caregiver burnout. . . . But nobody talks about how burnout creeps up on you, how it starts to happen before you even realize it. Burnout can be hard to recognize," says Celia Watson Seupel, who found herself filled with resentment and irritability after living with and caring for her elderly mother for more than a year.[11] She suddenly realized that she'd given up her morning prayer time and was, in fact, spiritually and emotionally exhausted.

"The experts say that caregivers must make time for themselves, but what I realized is how important the quality of that time is," she adds. "Time for oneself doesn't mean time working alone, even when it's work I love. It means taking time off to connect with friends, to have fun, and for me, most importantly, to renew from a wellspring deeper than my own."[12]

I'm fortunate that my mom realizes Mike and I need time away. She understands our need to see our grandchildren, even though she hates it when we're gone. If your parent uses guilt, manipulation, and judgment to keep you near, then learn to stand your ground. If your other relationships suffer because of lack of time together, communicate your expectations to your elderly loved one. Reassure your parent of your love. Remind him or her of any contingency plan for emergencies. Enlist the help of family or neighbors who will not only check in on your loved one, but also be there in case of a fall or an illness. Most important, remember to pray before, during, and after your conversation with your loved one.

Grace Growers

1. Review the list of burnout symptoms. When was the last time you took a break from caregiving? Although spontaneity may

not be an option, can you plan a time for yourself, doing something you enjoy?

2. Meditate on Philippians 4:13: "I can do all things through Christ who strengthens me" (NKJV). What does "all things" mean to you? Can you rest on His strength and resist feeling guilty about taking a respite?

PART III

———

ACCEPTING NEW ROLES

16

A DIFFERENT STATE
OF MIND

For who has known the mind of the Lord that he
may instruct him? But we have the mind of Christ.

1 CORINTHIANS 2:16

On Saturday I create the dinner menu for the week for
Mom, Mike, and me. Each week, I ask Mom the same
question.

"What would you like for dinner this week? Anything special?"

Each time, her answer is the same. "You decide. I don't want
to think about it."

We recently talked about supporting our daughter and her
husband as they prepare to work overseas as missionaries. Mom
wanted to send them money, but didn't know how much to send
on a monthly basis. "You decide," she told me.

As our parents age, they delegate more and more responsibility to their adult children. Often we slip into the parent role
without realizing it's happening. My mom has said repeatedly
that she doesn't want to have to make any more decisions. She

looks to Mike and me, and sometimes my brothers, for answers to questions such as these:

"Should I go through with this medical procedure?"

"Which air conditioning unit should I buy?"

"How much should I send to the great-grandkids for their birthdays?"

She added me to her checking account so I can pay her bills. She's given the doctor permission to share her medical history with me. She added Mike and me to her credit card and ordered new cards for us. At first, I was determined to dig in my heels and refuse to add Mom's financial affairs to my own. I was afraid of making late payments and angering her.

I've now come to see this as part of God's plan for me. It's another responsibility, certainly, and I need to be diligent. It's also a way for me to protect my mother from identity theft, phishing scams, and cyber financial crime. I work as a banker, and I know too well how easy it is to lose money to online thieves.

Sometimes I'm at a loss as I assume this responsibility for my own mother. How can I make sometimes life-altering decisions for *her*? I'm used to doing it for my children. God knows how many decisions we make between their conception and when we launch them into the world. They eventually make their own decisions, even if we think they're bad ones. We raise them to be independent and sigh with relief when they're on their own.

The new burden of responsibility for my mom rests even more heavily on my weary shoulders. On one side sits the angel, whispering, "You can do it. You'll be fine." On the other side is the dark one, accusing me of taking advantage. "Who do you think you are?" he rasps. "You're still a child. You can't make decisions for your mom."

Yet as parents begin to lose cognitive functioning, a role reversal that perhaps began slowly may shift into high gear. And as we make the shift to "parenting" our parents, the gears can often grind. It's not always a smooth transition. Our parents' minds are changing, but as caregivers, our minds will also need to change. We will need to find a different state of mind: the mind of Christ. Even though our parents' cognitive impairment may be frustrating, we will need to focus on Philippians 2:5: "Your attitude should be the same as that of Christ Jesus."

SIGNS OF DEMENTIA

Many times Mike or I have made a decision based on Mom's instruction, and then later have been challenged on it.

"I never told you to do that," she says.

Mike and I gently remind Mom of what she said, but she denies it. I cringe every time. Is this the beginning of the slow slide into dementia?

The terror of losing memory and function is a harsh reality among the elderly. Dementia, Alzheimer's disease, memory loss, and loss of functional ability can move your elderly parents back to a more childlike phase of life. How you respond to their fear—and any loss of function—will require more grace.

According to the Mayo Clinic, dementia is not one specific disease. It simply "describes a group of symptoms affecting memory, thinking and social abilities severely enough to interfere with daily functioning." Injury, stroke, several diseases, and even over- or under-medicating can bring about dementia.[1] Yet the leading cause of dementia is Alzheimer's disease, which causes changes in the brain and the progressive loss of mental ability.

Receiving a diagnosis of either chills to the bone, much like a diagnosis of cancer. Except unlike many forms of cancer, there's no cure. No wonder so many elderly people deny any loss of cognitive function, including my mother. A dementia diagnosis brings to mind drooling, slack-mouthed folks, lined up in nursing home hallways. For a generation of people with a deeply rooted belief in self-reliance, the idea being unable to communicate, feed themselves, or control their bodily functions is terrifying. Remember this as you talk with your parent; be gentle and don't condescend when you notice cognitive symptoms.

Trouble with memory can be an early sign of dementia, but a true dementia diagnosis requires at least two types of impairment that interfere with everyday life. Impairments in language, communication, focus, and reasoning all point to dementia, as do short-term memory changes. Other signs include difficulty finding the right words, mood changes, apathy, difficulty doing normal tasks, confusion, difficulty following story lines, a failing sense of direction, being repetitive, and struggling to adapt to change. Keep in mind that in addition to changes in the brain caused by Alzheimer's disease, a number of physical conditions and medications can affect a person's ability to communicate. Consult a doctor if you notice major changes.

If you suspect your loved one may be developing dementia, familiarize yourself with some of the common situations that arise when someone has these symptoms. That way if your loved one says something shocking, you'll know how to respond calmly and effectively. *Senior Living Blog* cites three common scenarios:

aggressive speech or actions, confusion about time or place, and poor judgment or cognitive problems.[2]

Knowing what to expect can make the difference between responding harshly and responding with grace. No one wants to be reminded of his or her diminishing memory. Whether your parent has dementia or Alzheimer's disease, reminding yourself that actual damage to the brain is causing your parent's aggression, confusion, or poor judgment may help you maintain an attitude of grace.

After my grandmother suffered a series of small strokes, she lost her short-term memory. At first, it was easy to remind her of things that happened the day before. Eventually, though, she forgot who I was. We'd chat for a few minutes, then she'd ask, "Now, who are you?"

I'd answer, "I'm Janie. Your granddaughter."

"Oh, yes, of course." She'd nod vigorously, as if she truly remembered, but I doubted it.

She was in a care facility by then, needing help for even her basic functions. Would Mom end up like that? What if she forgot me?

Every family has a secret language understood only by those in the circle. Shared memories and experiences bring code words that make us laugh or cry. Lines from movies and silly sayings become part of the fabric of the shared blanket of love that wraps around us like a warm cocoon. Mom and I share quotes from when I was younger. We know exactly what the other is saying when a particular phrase is uttered. We may see something on television, and it prompts a random comment. We giggle, leaving out everyone else in the room. We know what we mean, but the explanation just doesn't translate.

"You'd have to have been there" is Mom's response.

What would happen if all those shared memories disappear from Mom's mind? Where would I be? Would I flounder, unable to cope with her loss of brain function? Would I be one of the thousands of adult children who ask the question, "Where did my father/mother go?"

David's father, Marvin, suffers from dementia, and David and Maggie tried to deal with the problem on their own. When they finally realized Marvin needed more help than they could provide, David moved his father into a memory care facility. I asked him how Marvin was doing.

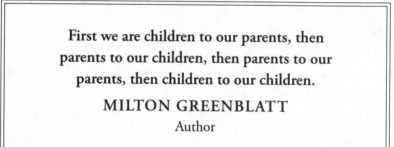

First we are children to our parents, then parents to our children, then parents to our parents, then children to our children.

MILTON GREENBLATT
Author

"He's doing really well," David reported. "Every morning he shows up at the facility staff meeting. The director welcomes him as part of the group. Dad's 'job' is to monitor the visitor log. He sits in the foyer all day, making sure visitors check in and out." What a relief it is for David and Maggie to know that Marvin feels useful.

If your father or mother has been diagnosed with Alzheimer's disease or dementia, spend some time on Alz.org. They have an excellent blog and resources such as local support groups. In the early stages of Alzheimer's disease, your loved one might still be able to live and function independently. As the disease progresses, however, his or her ability to handle daily tasks will dwindle.[3]

CONVERSING WITH GRACE

If you're dealing on your own with a parent diagnosed with memory loss, ongoing communication is important, no matter how difficult it may become or how confused the person with Alzheimer's or dementia may appear. You may need to remind your loved one of who you are. When I'd visit my grandmother after her stroke, I'd approach her and say, "Hi, Nini, it's me, Janie. Your granddaughter." Although she always said, "Of course I know who you are," many times I'd have to remind her again before the end of our visit.

Although Mom hasn't been diagnosed with dementia, I've noticed a loss of cognitive function. Her memory isn't as sharp as it used to be. She doesn't hear as well as she used to. Sometimes our conversations go something like this:

Me: Mike and I are going to a movie tonight.
Mom: Who's moving?
Me (louder): Mike and I—
Mom: You're moving?
Me: No, Mom. Mike and I are going to a movie tonight.
Mom: What are you going to see?
Me: *Jupiter Rising*.
Mom: Who's rising?

Or this:

> Mom: Did you make that transfer from savings to checking
>   I asked you to do?
> Me: No. When did you ask me?
> Mom: Last night at dinner.
> Me: No, you didn't ask me then.
> Mom: Yes, I did. You don't remember.

This is where Mike and I exchange a look. His expression says to let it go. It's a look we both use often.

The Bible says, "Listen to your father, who gave you life, and do not despise your mother when she is old" (Proverbs 23:22). Giving my mom the room to be right is a practical way I can obey this verse and offer grace to my mother. God wants me to let go of *my* need to be right.

Whether your parent has a mild cognitive impairment, dementia, or Alzheimer's disease, remember that God promises to provide all you need to "abound in every good work" (2 Corinthians 9:8). Your service to your elderly parents is definitely "good work," and God has the grace that you'll need during this difficult season.

Grace Growers

1. Meditate on Proverbs 23:22. How can you show honor to your elderly loved one in practical ways?
2. If your parent has been diagnosed with dementia or Alzheimer's disease, try to find someone who has walked in your shoes and can support you. And remember,

God is with you in your troubles. Isaiah 63:9 says, "In all their distress he too was distressed, and the angel of his presence saved them. In his love and mercy he redeemed them; he lifted them up and carried them all the days of old." Picture the Lord carrying you right now; ask Him to provide the support you need for grace-filled caregiving.

17

A TRAP OR A BLESSING?

As in nature, and in the arts, so in grace; it is rough
treatment that gives souls, as well as stones, their
lustre. The more the diamond is cut, the brighter
it sparkles, and in what seems hard dealing, God
has no end in view but to perfect our graces.

THOMAS GUTHRIE, CLERGYMAN AND PHILANTHROPIST

"Does June 1 mean anything to you?" The tone of my mom's
voice demands a quick response. I wrack my brain for
some event, some anniversary I may have missed.

"Um, no . . ." I answer, bracing for accusation.

"It's the day I'm able to ask for an increase in my widow's
benefits from the Veterans Administration."

Really? I was supposed to remember this? My stomach clenches
as my mom hands me a pile of papers, held together with an enormous jaw-like clip.

"These are all my medical expenses for the past year," she in-
forms me. "I need your help to fill out this Veterans Administration paperwork."

Translation: *You* need to fill out this paperwork.

I hide fluttering panic behind a nonchalant tone; I know the magnitude of this job.

"Sure. No problem. I'll take care of it."

As I carry out the tedious process of transferring prescriptions, doctor and dentist visits, medical supplies, hospital stays, and insurance costs to the VA form, I feel trapped in my caregiving role. Sometimes when I'm exhausted from interacting all day at work, making decisions, solving customer issues, and everything else involved in managing a bank, I don't feel like seeing my mom. Again, I can easily feel trapped by the constraints of caregiving.

THE VIEW FROM ABOVE

How we view our role as caregivers is important. Do we see it as a trap or a blessing? And whose validation do we seek as we do our work of caregiving?

I'll admit I like it when I talk to my friends about what I do for my mom.

"I cook dinner every night and take it down to my mom's house."

"Every night?" they ask.

"Yes, every night."

"You're a saint," they tell me. "I'd never do that."

Yes, I'm a martyr. A self-sacrificing, Proverbs 31 woman. A real Christian. Sometimes I enjoy my friends' validation. It's gratifying to have someone acknowledge the sacrifices I make. When someone tells me I'm a good person for sacrificing, it gives me a temporary lift and immediate gratification for a responsibility with few rewards other than intrinsic ones. Until God sharply reminds me not to look to man for affirmation.

When I care for my mother to gain validation from her and others, I become trapped in a spiritual way. The Bible says to do your work unto God, who will reward you. As I work through my motives for caregiving, I know that most of the time it feels good to give help, support, and joy to another person. Other times, I feel sorry for myself and grumble. Grumbling turns into resentment, and then bitterness and anger sow their weed-like seeds in my spirit. When I view caregiving as a trap, I need the Lord to help me examine my heart. If I don't continually take these feelings to the Lord in prayer, I can fall into sin, and that's the *real* trap. This is why it's important to hold the caregiving role with open hands before the Lord, examining our motives and looking to God for validation.

> **The opposite of sin is grace, not virtue.**
> **PHILIP YANCEY**
> Author

I picture myself carrying a backpack on a mountain trail. At first, the way is easy. My pack contains only what I'll need for the hike: some water, maybe nuts and raisins. If I were to throw a rock or two in the pack every few feet, by the time I reached the top of the trail I'd barely be able to put one foot in front of the other. I'd be carrying extra weight I didn't need to carry.

Have you ever seen someone so burdened down by emotions, they're literally bent over? Some carry guilt, others shame, and still others the top three—bitterness, unforgiveness, and resentment.

That's why I need Jesus. He said in Matthew 11:30, "My yoke is easy and my burden is light." It's a moment-by-moment choice to drop the burden of unhealthy emotions at His feet. Sometimes I need to find a place to be alone, consciously praying a prayer of release.

I encourage you to first ask for God's forgiveness for holding on to the emotions that have you bound. Then receive His complete cleansing, and watch how the burden can be shifted onto His shoulders. Sometimes this is a daily exercise for me. I have to forgive my brothers for not being there for Mom and Dad. I have to admit I'm tired and cranky and not in the mood to deal with them.

Each morning, I renew my spirit by putting aside the weights called selfishness, anger, and bitterness. These are the rocks I've tossed into my backpack on my journey. My prayer is that of our ultimate example, Jesus: "Not my will, but Thine be done."

It says very clearly in 1 John 3:16 how I should view my life: "This is how we know what love is: Jesus Christ laid down his life for us. And we ought to lay down our lives for our brothers." This is the attitude Jesus expects of me as I care for my aging loved ones.

I'd read in Andrew Murray's book, *Abide in Christ*, that God uses every situation in our life for His glory if we only let Him. I must be willing to let go of my own desires and allow God to transform me day by day as I help my mother in the few years she has remaining on the Earth.

CHOOSE THE BLESSING

As I look back, I realize that many blessings come from being the caregiver. I'm offered a glimpse into my parents' lives. They've shared funny stories about when my dad was stationed in Douglas, Arizona, during World War II, about their move to Spokane, Washington, and about their experiences building motels in Reno, Nevada. Their lives seem exciting and varied compared with mine. I've had the opportunity to hear their opinions on many subjects. I've been able to witness their joy as I drove them to Lake Tahoe or to Reno and away from the mundane schedule of their later lives. They could pretend for a little while that their lives hadn't changed, and I could too.

As I've gradually opened my heart to my new role of caretaker, of the "keeper of the folks," I've also received a rich reward of God's grace. I've learned that the caregiving season can be a time of spiritual growth for you and your aging loved one. Before you obtain this blessing, however, you can expect to feel growing pains. Remember Jesus' parable about the seed? It must fall to the earth and die before it can produce fruit. Dying to ourselves is painful, but the reward is new and beautiful fruit. And this fruit is my inheritance from my folks. The inheritance is not money, not real estate; it's the intangible blessing of being used by God.

The story of Isaac's inheritance from Abraham seems a perfect example of God's grace. "To [Isaac] he has given all that he has," Abraham's servant tells Rebekah in Genesis 24:36 (ESV). Isaac may not have wanted to assume the responsibility of caring for aging slaves and tending sick or lame cattle. But he did. It was all part of the inheritance from his father and his God. Not just the good stuff, but all the "bad" stuff too.

The inheritance of caregiving includes inconvenience, pain, and frustration. We don't have to accept our caregiving role, but we deny ourselves the good that may come from God if we do.

If we do accept this role, honor our parents, and place our total dependence on the Lord, God's grace is always available for us, allowing us to grow in spiritual maturity. View the responsibility of caregiving as an honor and privilege, and you'll find yourself growing more into the likeness of Christ.

Grace Growers

1. Consider Thomas Guthrie's statement at the beginning of this chapter. Each time you feel "trapped," can you view yourself as a diamond in progress? Ask God what He wants you to learn.

2. Where have bitterness and resentment crept into your spirit? Share with a partner, friend, or spiritual adviser, and ask them to pray with you and for you.

3. Meditate on Colossians 3:23. Think of your caregiving as work you are doing for the Lord. The following verse says, "It is the Lord Christ you are serving." As you do your caregiving tasks, picture Jesus in place of your loved one.

18

MARRIAGE AND CAREGIVING

For this reason a man will leave his father
and mother and be united to his wife,
and they will become one flesh.

GENESIS 2:24

We don't cook on Thursday nights. Mike and I have a Bible study in our home that evening, and we spend the time between work and 7:00 p.m. preparing the house, making coffee, setting out plates, and reading the Scripture verses. We call it "Fend Night." Fend for yourself. Mom understands that we don't deliver dinner on Thursdays.

One evening we mentioned to Mom that we would also like to take Sundays off from preparing dinner. Mike and I wanted to have one night a week when we could sit across the table from each other, in our own home, by ourselves.

Mom came unglued.

"Not have Sunday dinner together? We always have Sunday dinner!" She got up from the table, grabbed her walker, and shuffled down the hall to her bedroom.

"Where are you going?" Mike asked her.

"To my room to cry."

Mom's half-eaten dinner accused me from the flowered plate.

Mike shook his head. "Maybe I should have worded it differently."

I waited a moment and then headed down the hall, my stomach in knots. Mom sat on the edge of the bed, tissue pressed to her eyes.

"You two are so good to me," she told me as I patted her back. "I shouldn't complain."

"So you're saying you're upset because Mike and I want to have a dinner at home alone?"

"Yes," she replied. "I'm sorry, but it's all about me right now."

I finally coaxed her back to the kitchen, but neither of us had any appetite. Mike tried to talk about why we wanted time alone, but she wouldn't hear it. He asked if it would be easier if we didn't do dinner on Saturday instead. She refused to talk.

"Don't make me cry again," she said.

I wanted to crawl in a hole. I couldn't please anyone, not even myself. If I indulged in an intimate dinner with Mike, I'd feel guilty for leaving Mom at home alone. If I gave up that desire, Mike would be frustrated. Mom knows where all of Mike's "buttons" are, and she pushes every single one. He needed a break from her as much as I did.

JUST THE TWO OF US

Mike and I have a saying: "I just want to play with my sister." We picked it up from our time as missionary pastors in Montana. There was a family living across the street with two boys around our son's age. Justin and Kevin would knock on the door, asking if Bobby could play. If Bobby and his sister were having fun together, he'd tell them, "No, I just want to play with my sister." It became our code. If one of us wants to invite someone over or do something with another couple but the other doesn't want to, the response is, "I just want to play with my sister." That's how we feel about having dinner together, just the two of us, one night a week.

In her book *Mother Daughter Me*, Katie Hafner tells of her life after asking her elderly mother to move in with her and her daughter, Zoe. Katie and Zoe had a close relationship after Katie's husband died. When Katie's mother moved in, the fabric of their relationship couldn't stretch to include her.

> My mother is thinking the same thing. We're seated at the kitchen table, she with her decaf-Splenda concoction, I with a cup of regular coffee. We agree that we cannot live together. The immediate and face-saving reason we agree upon is physical. Her knee is giving her a lot of trouble, and each trip up and down the stairs of the house has become a painful chore. But she and I also know that, for all three of us, the emotional effluvium is contaminating the very air we breathe.[1]

Keep in mind that any disruption in a longstanding family pattern—a disruption of the "family system"— can be difficult for everyone, including the care receiver.

AGINGCARE.COM

Sometimes I feel the same way. Mike and I have been empty nesters since 1999. Our daughter, Heather, married a few months after Bobby graduated from high school and moved out of state to live with his uncle. For fifteen years we went where we wanted to go, when we wanted to go. We ate dinner at eight o'clock, or not at all. This gradual slide into more responsibility has sometimes tested the bounds of our patience with each other.

As I struggle with the dilemma of honoring my mother (Exodus 20:12), and honoring my husband (Colossians 3:18), I must ask God for wisdom. When I feel emotionally blackmailed by my mother, God is the only One who can help me see past the dark mist swirling in my heart and mind. Sometimes the answer is in the form of advice from a friend who has faced a similar situation. Other times, God gives me the wisdom I desperately seek as I read His Word.

Mike becomes frustrated with Mom because of her never-ending "honey-do" lists written on yellow sticky notes. It irritates him. Then it irritates me, because he's irritated. I'm also irritated because he'll tell her, "I'll do these on Saturday." I wanted him to do stuff at *our* house on Saturday. I mentally crush *my* to-do list and swallow it like a dry cotton ball.

Mom's weeds are pulled, garden raked, roses fed, lightbulbs changed, and leaky showerhead fixed. The only thing growing in my garden is weeds. The bathroom is dark, and the showerhead drips. I feel like the second wife. When I complain to Mike, he feels the tension of our three-person family. Like me, he's caught in the middle.

When caring for an aging loved one, the question is often

asked, "Whose needs come first?" This is my question. Should Mom come first, since she's unable to care for herself? Or should Mike, as my life partner, come first?

"The relationship between husband and wife trumps everything else," says Dr. Charles Schmitz, who with his wife, Elizabeth, authored *Golden Anniversaries: The Seven Secrets of Successful Marriage.* "If they continue to strengthen their relationship with each other, their marriage will survive the enormous challenges associated with caring for aging parents."[2]

It's vital to keep your marriage a priority while caregiving. Experts agree that communication is key in reducing stress in your relationship while caring for an aging loved one. Too often, one or both spouses become overwhelmed and shut down. Therapist Bobbi Emel urges caregiving couples to meet regularly to express their feelings, talk about practical matters, and simply vent. "It's important, for example, to have an understanding that it's okay to express your frustrations or convey how exhausting your week was," she says.[3]

Karen Sherman, therapist and author of *Marriage Magic! Find It, Keep It, and Make It Last,* agrees that time alone and sharing feelings is important. "Really let your feelings come out," she urges. "Don't feel guilty about expressing them. Don't keep emotions pent up. Clearly, care for parents or an ill spouse is extremely stressful."[4]

This is where things get real. Mike and I must be able to not only talk about our own needs with each other, but also discuss our needs with Mom, regardless of her tears. John Townsend and Henry Cloud, authors of the book *Boundaries,* discuss how to set boundaries with every relationship, including our parents:

As an adult, loving and honoring your parents does not equal obeying. . . . While you are to respect and care for your parents, you are no longer under their protection and tutelage. Children are to obey parents, while adult children are to love and honor them. Therefore, sometimes you will need to confront parents, disobeying their desire for you to agree with them or go along with a bad situation."[5]

Don't hesitate to seek marriage counseling if needed. We benefited from counseling around year ten, after we had already agreed that divorce would never be an option. After returning to California from a three-year mission call to rural Montana, more counseling followed as we struggled to assimilate back into an urban environment. Sometimes our arguments escalated into shouting. We were both unhappy, so we met with a counselor who specialized in pastoral burnout. I discovered that my identity had been rooted in being the perfect pastor's wife. Mike also struggled because he wasn't able to find full-time ministry work. Both identity issues affected our relationship. After counseling, our marriage took a huge leap forward. Honest communication was difficult to learn, but I thank God we did.

After our son died, most of the little things that used to irritate me about Mike didn't seem important anymore. Seeing him grieve over Bobby made me love him even more. We've been through many seasons in our thirty-eight years of marriage. We've seen financial ups and downs; we've watched our children stray from the Lord, then return. Mike nursed me through cancer treatment. We felt the pain and frustration of seeing foster children returned to unhealthy family situations, unable to prevent it. As I consider our history together, I realize that caregiving for Mom is just another season in our marriage. It will pass.

KULEANA

At a Christian conference I attended, a speaker used a Hawaiian word I'd never heard before: *kuleana*. It means a responsibility, but it's more than a duty or "task." It also carries a connotation of privilege. I wondered if I could apply this to caring for my mother. Could I adjust my perspective and view this responsibility as a privilege?

As I struggle through the emotions and disappointments in my relationship with my mother, God continues to remind me that it's a privilege to care for her. When I'm able to lay aside my hurt, He's able to change my perspective. I no longer look at Mom as an intruder into my relationship with Mike. I can again see her as a person with expectations and disappointments of her own. I can grow beyond the child who stamps her foot to get her own way. I can put myself in Mom's place and empathize with her, while firmly creating space for my husband.

God is helping me see my mother as a person with her own emotional ups and downs. I don't know what it's like to watch my friends become sick and die. I can't imagine being ninety-one and wondering when it will be my turn. As I continue to view my mother in a new light, my capacity for offering grace continues to grow.

I'm also learning to look for the silver lining in my situation. Sometimes Mike and I find something to celebrate with my mother. We'll prepare a special dinner and spend more than just a half hour at her house, celebrating something as simple as my success at landing a good account at work. We also celebrate my dad's birthday or the anniversary of his death. Mom appreciates our acknowledgement of these important days and being a part of our lives.

NEGOTIATING

Mike decided that instead of being irritated by Mom's "honey-do" list, he'd face the frustration head-on.

"How about I come over Saturday morning and get as much done on this list as possible?" he asked Mom. "The afternoon is all Jane's. I have things to get done at home, too."

"What if you don't finish all my tasks?" Mom wanted to know.

Mike shrugged. "I'll get to them when I can."

Mom agreed. Since then, whenever there's a yellow sticky note next to Mike's placemat, he asks Mom for a deadline.

"Does it need to be done today? This week? Before the end of the month?"

I wish I could say it's solved the problem entirely. Nevertheless, Mike's irritation and my resentment have mostly been resolved.

After Mom's meltdown, she realized that Mike and I needed time alone. It turns out that on the day we mentioned having Sunday dinner as a couple, Mom had visited with an old friend, Margie, who was in a convalescent hospital following a stroke. Margie was depressed and in quite a bit of pain. Mom had come home upset and discouraged after trying to share Jesus with Margie, who couldn't understand what Mom was saying. Our "announcement" had come at a bad time, and that affected my mother's response. *I've outlived my usefulness*, she thought.

Even my daughter doesn't want me around. That's what she heard, though that's not what was said.

I'm thankful our relationship can withstand the occasional meltdown. We agreed that Saturday nights would be a date night for Mike and me. Sometimes we go to dinner and a movie, other times we rent a movie and eat dinner in front of the television. Mom has accepted this as the new routine.

As you learn to accept your unique caregiving role and negotiate boundaries, make sure that you set aside time to have fun with your spouse. Regular date nights and days away just to unwind will strengthen your marriage and keep your relationship in first place. Mike and I love going out for frozen yogurt. After a long day at work and then preparing dinner for Mom, we'll look at each other and say, "Fro yo?" Sitting outside the yogurt shop away from the four walls of our house gives us a chance to talk without distraction. We agree to leave our cell phones in the car. Sometimes we just "people watch." It's a mini-date, but it refreshes our spirits, readying us for the next *kuleana.*

Grace Growers
1. How has caregiving affected your marriage? What boundaries have you set on your responsibility for your loved one's needs so you can be alone with your spouse?
2. With your spouse, brainstorm ways to have respite together from caregiving. Where are you finding your support system these days? Could it use some bolstering?
3. Meditate on Genesis 2:24. Use this caregiving season as an opportunity to grow spiritually with your spouse. Pray together for your marriage and for your aging loved ones.

4. What is your *kuleana*? Today ask, *Is this my responsibility?*
   And if it is, tell yourself: *I am privileged to be the person
   tasked with this.*

PART IV

EXITING WITH GRACE

19

END-OF-LIFE DECISIONS

There is a time for everything,
and a season for every activity under heaven.

ECCLESIASTES 3:1

The number of Americans living to age 100 has grown by an astounding 66 percent since 1980, thanks to advances in medicine and disease treatment.[1] While medical advancements have enabled people to live longer, with age also comes an increase in the number of elderly who need assistance with their basic daily needs.[2] As our loved ones' needs increase, we must talk with them about housing and care options and, as hard as it is, about how they wish to die. As Christian caregivers, we're called upon to make difficult decisions for our parents as they near the end of their lives.

My ninety-one-year-old mother is determined to die in her own home. I see someone who is stuck inside four walls, fearful of going outside. She values her independence. I worry she'll set the house on fire because she's forgotten to turn off the stove.

Ironically, she says she doesn't want to be a burden to anyone, yet she chooses to ignore the emotional wear and tear on Mike and me. If her window blinds are still closed when I drive by her place on my way to work, I wonder, *Is everything okay?* I suppose it's less of a blow to her pride if she thinks strangers don't have to help her.

When we talked to my dad about moving into a board-and-care home, we considered the impact on the entire family, not just on him. Some questions we discussed with an eldercare advocate were: How long could my mother continue to monitor my father's health? How much would a board-and-care home cost, compared with a home health nurse and the cost of an emergency room visit? What if no one in the immediate family was available to help if Dad or Mom had a medical emergency?

As difficult as the decision was to move Dad, my father realized that living at home was hard on Mom. Now Mike and I talk about when we might need to move Mom, too.

HOUSING OPTIONS

There are people on both sides of the housing debate: those who believe that the best option is letting their parents stay in their homes as long as possible, and those who think aging at home is dangerous and more costly.

Margie is a friend of mine who takes care of her mom and mother-in-law. Both elderly women are determined to die in their own homes as well. It's easy to see how it seems like the natural order of things. After all, didn't Grandma and Grandpa Walton live in a downstairs bedroom in the rambling Walton home on that old TV show?

For a three-year period when I was a child, my grandparents lived with us, and I don't remember it as being difficult or causing strife. We had a big enough house that they had their own room, as did both of my brothers, so we coexisted comfortably.

For many couples, however, adding a parent to their home would be uncomfortable at best. That would be true for Mike and me. But if we were to lose a job, we might not have the luxury of maintaining our house and Mom's. Some baby boomers have boomerang kids: the high school or college graduates who left home as young adults only to return as the economy soured. Adding elderly parents to such a household has its own set of challenges.

Before you know what's best for your parents and your family, "you need to know exactly where your parents stand physically and mentally, and then combine this information with their personal preferences," says Nancy Parker Brummett in her book *Take My Hand Again: A Faith-Based Guide for Helping Aging Parents*. A physical assessment by a doctor who practices geriatrics is best, she advises, followed by a neurological assessment in order to reveal any element of dementia or cognitive decline that may weigh in on the issue.[3]

Once you have that information, it's easier to know what level of care your loved one needs, how soon those needs might change, and whether in-home care, such as a visiting nurse, will suffice. It's also good to answer a few questions as honestly as possible: Will my parents feel comfortable with an outside person helping with day-to-day care? Am I capable of handling my role in this type of care? Will this type of care affect my own personal well-being?

Housing choices providing some care include assisted-living arrangements that help people stay as independent as possible. AARP suggests, "There are also 'board-and-care homes' and 'personal care group homes,' which are single-family dwellings licensed at the state or local level to provide care. They offer meals, activities, housekeeping, transportation, and some level of security."[4]

Nursing homes, also known as skilled nursing facilities, have aides and skilled nurses on hand twenty-four hours a day. Since the quality of nursing homes can vary widely, it's wise to carefully research your choice if your parent needs this type of medical care.

Continuing-care retirement communities are another option, providing whatever level of care is needed. Such facilities "feature independent-living apartments and homes, and offer the various social, recreational, and cultural activities of other retirement communities. But they also have assisted-living and nursing-level care. In this 'continuum-of-care' system, residents usually enter the facility at the independent-living level. Later, if their health and abilities decline, they can move to the [on-site] assisted-living tier, and then, if necessary, to the nursing-home tier."[5]

FACING THE FUTURE

As you consider your parents' needs and the options available, you might find yourself asking this question: How do I show my parents respect and honor while in essence taking away their independence? The answer is to continue conversing with our loved ones while being honest and facing reality.

"I just want my life back," my mom says. She wants to turn the clock back to her prior pain-free existence, a time when her husband was alive and they were healthy enough to go out for hot fudge sundaes. She wants the life she had before hearing loss, debilitating health problems, and blindness left her feeling trapped by her physical limitations. A loss of control, shrinking boundaries, and fears can make life difficult for an aging loved one. It can be excruciating for them to watch friends become ill, disabled, and weak. Attending friends' funerals can be especially difficult for our parents when they are able to number their remaining friends on one hand.

It's easy to understand why your loved one (and maybe you, too) may hope that life will one day "return to normal." Yet when our parents' needs have overtaken our ability to adequately care for them, we must be frank, even though it's difficult. For the sake of all involved, sentimentality or wishful thinking should not obscure the reality of aging.

The caretaker role may eventually require us to make gut-wrenching decisions. I know that time will once again come for me. My mother has fallen several times because she can't see large cracks in the sidewalk. Even with a walker, she worries she'll tumble. When we walk together and I hold her arm, her steps are halting, and I worry I won't be able to keep her from falling. And if she does fall and needs to be hospitalized, would I be able to support her living at home? I shudder at the thought of discussing assisted living with my mom. She'll likely dig in her heels, and I can't blame her. I wouldn't want to be forced to leave my home. Most seniors don't. It's a delicate and touchy subject.

My friend Gary cares for his mom in his home. He says it's been a six-month process preparing his mother to move into an assisted-living facility. Her care has gone beyond what he can provide while working full time and running a mentoring program for at-risk youth. Gary and his wife started by dropping hints to his mother. Then they had "the talk." Finally, they toured several facilities. I asked Gary the other day if they'd moved his mom yet.

"No, she's still clinging to the doorjambs. I think we'll have to pry her out with a can opener," he said with a chuckle.

My coworker Janet returned from a business trip to find her seventy-four-year-old mother suddenly exhibiting signs of severe dementia. The woman called Janet several times during the day, yelling about the lack of response from the doctor's office. Her behavior went steadily downhill from there. She thought people were spying on her from the television and didn't recognize her own husband. Was it a stroke? Was she overmedicated? Did she have an undetected urinary tract infection, which can cause confusion, falls, incontinence, and a decrease in appetite?

Following more bizarre behavior and a call to 9-1-1 about a suspected kidnapping, Janet was forced to act. Her eighty-year-old father could not advocate for his wife's care, and Janet had no training in dealing with Medicare, mental health issues, hospital staff, and doctors. Janet and her brother made the decision to move their mom to a facility where she could be evaluated for psychological problems.

My mom may be granted her wish to die in her own home, but that may change if she has a stroke or another medical condition that requires a higher level of care. For now, we've found a situation that works as well as we can hope. I want to do all I can to honor my mother's wishes to stay in her home until she passes, as I see how much she enjoys puttering around her little townhome, endlessly baking.

HIGH-TECH HELP

Mom and I discussed installing sensors on her refrigerator and the floor by her bed, a high-tech way to monitor her while she maintains her independence. With an app on my phone, I would know if she got out of bed and made it to the kitchen. It would be peace of mind for both of us. If she fell, I'd be aware before I left work, and I wouldn't have to worry seeing that her blinds were still closed when I left in the morning. We're discussing this solution, while being sensitive to Mom's need for privacy.

"It's like a baby monitor," she's complained. I agree, but baby monitors are there for a good reason. Before installing sensors, caregivers need to have a frank talk with their loved ones about privacy and how much help they need.

"Advances in low-cost sensors and wireless networks are fueling a boom in the so-called 'smart home,'" reports Brandon Bailey of the Associated Press. "And companies are looking beyond home security and temperature control to creating products for Baby Boomers trying to balance caring for aging parents and respecting their independence."[6]

Such technology is just one example of the so-called "aging in place" movement driven by baby boomers like me, who have aging parents to keep an eye on. Other systems integrate webcams and video conferencing systems with the Internet and report to you, your computer, or a dispatcher if something is out of the ordinary. There are even gadgets to remind the elderly to take their medication. This advance can mean the difference between living at home or in a nursing facility, since the inability to take medication unsupervised accounts for up to 40 percent of nursing home admissions.[7] One of these automatic pill reminders stores a month of medication and sounds an alarm when it's time to take the pills; another reminds you if you've missed a dose. There are also services that will send your parents medication reminders by phone, e-mail, or pager. Devices that keep the shower water temperatures from scalding your loved one and those that will shut off a stove burner at a certain temperature can give caregivers peace of mind.

FINAL WISHES

As our parents reach their final days, decisions also must be made about their final wishes. Most of the time, parents have the leisure to talk about passing on their material goods. After my dad died, my mom gave away her jewelry—some to me, and some to my two sisters-in-law. She gave up her china, silverware, and crystal. She didn't want any arguments after she was gone.

One especially difficult discussion to have with our aging loved one is about the funeral or memorial service. Mike and I have talked with my mother several times about her memorial service, asking her questions about who we should invite to give the eulogy, and which songs, hymns, and Scriptures she wants included. I'm grateful she's willing to discuss it, as difficult as it is.

Some aren't so blessed. RemnantReport.com describes families arguing even as the loved one is being lowered into the ground. "Emotions are raw and vulnerable during funerals. All of the past feelings of success and failure relating to the deceased seem to come out in the survivors after a person has died. This can cause bitter feelings and ugly fights which can last a lifetime."[8]

That's another reason for siblings to gather and talk with their parents about these decisions while they can. It allows an opportunity for siblings to weigh in, which should minimize possible memorial service meltdowns. Making sure my brothers have a part in planning Mom's service has helped open the lines of communication between us. My oldest brother, Dean, has been more attentive to Mom now that he's realized her frailty.

Another end-of-life issue is whether your parent wants a Do Not Resuscitate order, or DNR. This document helps an elderly or terminally ill person ensure death with dignity. It alerts medical personnel that the individual does not want to receive CPR or electric shock should breathing cease or his heart stop. Your aging loved one's doctor can help explain the pros and cons of a DNR. My folks decided early on that a DNR was the right choice for them.

What if your parents don't want a DNR? They may wish to take advantage of every lifesaving measure should they suffer a heart attack or stroke. In this case, it is imperative to have a discussion prior to a life-altering event.

We received tremendous peace of mind by hiring an attorney who specializes in elder law. Instead of being charged by the hour, we paid a set amount to set up a family trust and a durable power of attorney for health care, which included an Advance Medical Directive. My parents' wishes are spelled out in these documents.

Having an advance health care directive (a.k.a. power of attorney for health care) allows you to name someone you trust to make decisions regarding your health care at a time when you are unable to do so for yourself, explains elder law attorney Lawrence Solorio.

"In addition, this document allows you to list various specific end of life wishes that you want your agents to carry out on your behalf," he says. "You don't want the Court appointing a health care agent for you . . . it's your life . . . so plan for it."⁹

I've found it's helpful to break the discussions about these issues into small chunks. You may want to begin with a question such as this: "Mom, Dad, have you thought about what you'll do when you can't live at home anymore?" It's likely they have thought about and already discussed it. Ask permission to be a part of their conversation.

After they and you have had time to digest that, try asking, "Are you familiar with a Do Not Resuscitate order?" Chances are they know what it is, but they may not know how to go about getting one. This is where a family doctor can help, as he or she will have to sign the form.

Another small chunk of conversation can begin like this: "Dad, have you made arrangements for your finances if something happens to you? Mom, same question." Your loved one may not be willing at this point to talk about finances. Be patient, but persistent. These issues won't disappear if you ignore them.

To prepare for these conversations, you may want to list the challenges you're facing concerning end-of-life decisions for your loved one and give them some thought. You may consider questions such as:

> Do I live close enough to help my parent in a crisis? If not, can or will my siblings step up?
> Do I have the financial means to help defray the cost of end-of-life care or conveniences to help my parent stay at home until they pass?
> Can I be flexible as my loved one's needs change?

I remember when my son was a toddler, and he'd climbed up on the counter to snatch some cookies that I'd just baked. I discovered him sitting on the kitchen floor, hands and face smeared with chocolate and crumbs.

"What did you do?" I demanded. He closed his eyes, believing that if he couldn't see me, I couldn't see him.

Sometimes I think we do the same thing as adults. I wish I could close my eyes and make these difficult decisions go away. My brain knows that won't happen, but my heart needs preparation to deal with my mother's final days. God can help us prepare our hearts for these difficult conversations if we simply ask for His help.

Grace Growers

1. Think of some times, places, or specific situations that will allow you to begin an end-of-life discussion with your mom or dad. What specifics need discussing? What might your plan look like?

2. Meditate on Ecclesiastes 3:1. Think about how the caregiving season has changed you. Be willing to let your loved one go, knowing you've given them love and grace.

FINAL THOUGHTS

I'm sitting in Mom's living room. It's Sunday afternoon and we're waiting for Mike to come home from a day of golf. Dinner is simmering on the stove. Mom and I are sharing some munchies and a drink, chatting about this and that, and feeling relaxed. There's no agenda, no yellow sticky notes with things to do, no stack of bills Mom wants me to pay.

My mind wanders back to what it was like before my parents grew old. My dad never said the words "I love you," yet he showed me in countless ways. When he got home from work, he'd empty the change from his pockets onto my bed. One day he brought home a small television for me to put in my room. He'd traded something for it. I was the only kid on my block with my own TV.

My mom and I were constant companions growing up. After giving birth to two boys, she was thrilled to have a girl. Twice a year we went on a shopping trip to San Francisco to buy clothes for the new season. She took me to plays and concerts to broaden my horizon; she taught me to cook and to clean. People say I look just like her. Sometimes when I catch a glimpse of myself passing a mirror, I have to agree.

I wasn't born into this family by accident. God knew exactly what He was doing when He placed me third in the birth order. His grace brought me to being the caregiver, and His grace will carry me through this season if I allow Him to. As I've journeyed through my parents' process of aging and dying, I've learned to accept and bestow more and more of God's grace. Caring for the ones who raised you can be a rich and rewarding experience if you allow God to help you appreciate the heritage you've been given as children of the Greatest Generation. Our parents have lived through some tough times: the Great Depression, World War II, the Korean War, food and gas rationing. We come from hardy stock!

Yes, the caregiving season can be emotionally and physically exhausting, but like all seasons, it doesn't last forever. The leaves will fall; the snow will cover the ground and later melt away, bringing the fresh, new growth of springtime. Decide with God that your caregiving season will end with your own new spiritual growth.

And consider this: At some point all of us may require the same amount of grace-filled caregiving. Can we learn about aging gracefully ourselves as we tend to our parents? As one seventy-eight-year-old woman says, "Middle-aged people need the elderly, although they may not know it or even believe it. To grow older themselves, younger people need the lessons that can be learned only from caring for their parents."[1]

As I look toward my parentless future, I'm grateful for the time my mom and I have had together. As Frank Sinatra sang,

"Regrets, I've had a few." I'm not a perfect caregiver. Sometimes my selfishness rears up and obscures my vision of the eternal value I'm providing. But I know I've brought joy into the lives of the two people who made it possible for me to be alive.

May you find grace to sustain you in caring for your elderly loved one. Remember *kuleana*. It's an honor and a privilege to give care to another. Just as Jesus humbled Himself to wash His disciples' feet, so humble yourself. Embrace all God has for you in this final season of your parents' lives.

ACKNOWLEDGMENTS

To my husband, friend, partner, and cheerleader. Mike, you make me proud to be your wife. Thank you for your encouragement during the process of writing our story.

This book wouldn't have been written without the help of my writing coach and editor extraordinaire, Mick Silva. You made me work hard and dig deep. Thank you.

Thanks to my writing sisters in Inspire Christian Writers. Whenever I uttered the words, "I can't write," you reminded me of God's grace. Love and cheese, ladies.

To the editorial staff at Focus on the Family, especially Julie Holmquist, a huge thank-you. Larry Weeden, thanks for going to bat for me and helping me expand on my original idea.

Finally, I want to thank the best parents on Earth, Roger and Charleen. It is an honor and privilege to be your daughter. I'm glad I've had the chance to give back a tiny portion of what you've given me.

To God be the glory. Amen.

NOTES

INTRODUCTION
1. Rob Lowe, "To Start the New Year Right Have 'The Talk' with Your Aging Parents," *CNN Opinion*, February 6, 2015, http://www.cnn.com/2015/01/12 /health/feat-rob-lowe-aging-parents.
2. "A Profile of Older Americans: 2012," Administration on Aging, Administration for Community Living, U.S. Department of Health and Human Services.

CHAPTER 1: SEEING THE SIGNS
1. Marlo Sollitto, "20 Warning Signs That an Elder Is an Unsafe Driver," Agingcare, https://www.agingcare.com/Articles/signs-elder-unsafe-driver-153264.htm.
2. "Older Adult Drivers," Centers for Disease Control and Prevention, May 27, 2015, http://www.cdc.gov/Motorvehiclesafety/Older_Adult_Drivers/index.html.
3. "Reasons Why Teenagers and Older People Are the Riskiest Drivers," *Consumer Reports*, October 2012, http://www.consumerreports.org/cro/magazine/2012/10 /teenagers-and-older-people-are-the-riskiest-drivers/index.htm.

CHAPTER 2: DAD, CAN I HAVE THE CAR KEYS?
1. Paula Span, "Suicide Rates Are High among the Elderly," *New York Times*, August 7, 2013.
2. Ibid.
3. Helen H. Lemmel, "Turn Your Eyes upon Jesus," 1922, Public Domain.

CHAPTER 3: WHAT HAPPENED TO MY DAD?
1. "Seniors and Chronic Pain," *NIH Medline Plus*, Fall 2011, 15.
2. *2015 Alzheimer's Disease Fact and Figures* (Chicago, IL: Alzheimer's Association, 2015), 35.

3. Peter Rosenberger, *Hope for the Caregiver* (Brentwood, TN: Worthy Inspired, 2014), 60.

CHAPTER 4: CALLING 9-1-1 AGAIN

1. Flora Maloney (coordinator, The Club Senior Day Care, Rancho Cordova, CA), in interview with author, February 11, 2015.

CHAPTER 5: GETTING OLD IS MESSY

1. William E. Whitehead, "Understanding Fecal Incontinence," University of North Carolina Center for Functional GI & Motility Disorders, https://www.med.unc.edu/ibs/files/educational-gi-handouts/Understanding%20Fecal%20 Incontinence.pdf.
2. Henry Holstege and Robert Riekse, eds., *Complete Guide to Caring for Aging Loved Ones* (Carol Stream, IL: Tyndale House/Focus on the Family, 2002), 194.
3. "Nearly Half a Million Americans Suffered from Clostridium Difficile Infections in a Single Year," Centers for Disease Control and Prevention, press release, February 25, 2015, http://www.cdc.gov/media/releases/2015/p0225 -clostridium-difficile.html.
4. Darshan Shah and Gopal Badlani, "Treatment of Overactive Bladder and Incontinence in the Elderly," *Reviews in Urology* 4 suppl. 4 (2002): S38–S43.
5. John Piper, "Grace Is Pardon—and Power!" *Solid Joys: Daily Devotionals by John Piper*, http://solidjoys.desiringgod.org/en/devotionals/grace-is-pardon-and -power.
6. Emma Innes, "The 'Old Age' Suit Being Used to Teach Hospital Staff How It Feels to Be Elderly," DailyMail.com, March 5, 2014, http://www.dailymail .co.uk/health/article-2573779/Deafness-shaking-hands-shuffling-The-old-age -suit-used-teach-hospital-staff-feels-elderly.html.

CHAPTER 6: HOW TO SAY GOOD-BYE

1. Gerald Sittser, *A Grace Disguised: How the Soul Grows Through Loss* (Grand Rapids, MI: Zondervan, 1995), 164.
2. Connie Matthiessen, "Talking to a Loved One About Death," Caring.com, https://www.caring.com/articles/talking-to-a-dying-parent.
3. Ibid.
4. Kate Ashford, "12 Tough Questions to Ask Your Parents," *CBS Money Watch*, September 2, 2009, http://www.cbsnews.com/news/12-tough-questions-to -ask-your-parents/.

CHAPTER 7: MAY I BE FRANK?

1. Marilyn Sharbach Ladew, "Ten Secrets That Aging Parents Keep," Agingcare, https://www.agingcare.com/Articles/elderly-keeping-secrets-from-their-family -133477.htm.

2. David B. Oliver, "The Real Caregivers in the Nursing Home: Certified Nursing Assistants," *Bioethics Forum*, Fall 1999, 21, http://practicalbioethics.org/files /members/documents/Oliver_15_3.pdf.

CHAPTER 8: SIBLING RIVALRY
1. Bonnie Lawrence, "A Sibling's Guide to Caring for Aging Parents," *PBS Newshour*, November 28, 2014, http://www.pbs.org/newshour/updates/youre -sharing-care-aging-parents.
2. Holstege and Riekse, *Caring for Aging Loved Ones*, 54.
3. Francine Russo, "Caregiving with Your Siblings," Family Caregiver Alliance Fact Sheet, 2011, https://www.caregiver.org/caregiving-with-your-siblings.

CHAPTER 9: THE LINE IN THE SAND
1. John Shore, "Fifteen Ways to Stay Sane While Caring for an Elderly Parent," *Huffington Post*, February 18, 2011, http://huffingtonpost.com/john-short/elderly -parent-caregivers_b_823443.html.
2. Zanda Hilger, "Behavior and Emotions of Aging," Family Caregivers Online, Area Agency on Aging, 2009, http://www.familycaregiversonline.net/online -education/behavior-and-emotions-of-aging/.
3. Ibid.

CHAPTER 10: NOURISHING BODY AND SOUL
1. "How to Prevent Senior Malnutrition," A Place for Mom, 2015, http://www .aplaceformom.com/nutrition.
2. "Depression in the Elderly," WebMD, April 4, 2016, http://www.webmd.com /depression/guide/depression-elderly.
3. "Depression in Older Persons," National Alliance on Mental Illness Fact Sheet, 2009, http://www.namihelps.org/Depression_Older_Persons.pdf.
4. Ibid.
5. "Research Suggests a Positive Correlation between Social Interaction and Health," National Institute on Aging, https://www.nia.nih.gov/about/living -long-well-21st-century-strategic-directions-research-aging/research-suggests -positive.

CHAPTER 11: LETTING GO OF EXPECTATIONS
1. Taryn Benson (Senior Care Solutions, Inc.), in interviews with author, October 31, 2014, and January 26, 2015.
2. Marjorie S. Miller, "Communication Is Key When Dealing with Aging Parents," *Penn State News*, January 27, 2015, http://news.psu.edu/story /342263/2015/01/27/research/communication-key-when-dealing-aging -parents.
3. Holstege and Riekse, *Caring for Aging Loved Ones*, 64, 66.

CHAPTER 12: GUILTY OR NOT GUILTY?

1. Rosenberger, *Hope for the Caregiver*, 209.
2. Benson interviews, 2014 and 2015.
3. "A Guide to Taking Care of Yourself," Family Caregiver Alliance, January 1, 2012, https://www.caregiver.org/guide-taking-care-yourself.
4. Holstege and Riekse, *Caring for Aging Loved Ones*, 72–73.

CHAPTER 13: HEART CARE

1. Jim Daly, "Forgiveness Key to Caring for Elderly Parents," Uexpress, July 21, 2013, http://www.uexpress.com/focus-on-the-family/2013/7/21/forgiveness -key-to-caring-for-elderly.
2. Nancy Parker Brummett, *Take My Hand Again: A Faith-Based Guide For Helping Aging Parents* (Grand Rapids, MI: Kregel Publications, 2015), 188–189.
3. Mark Goulston, "The Eldercaring Challenge: Caring for a Difficult Parent," *Psychology Today*, April 28, 2010.
4. Lori Hogan, *Strength for the Moment: Inspiration for Caregivers* (New York: Image, 2012), 25–26.
5. Martha Stettinius, "I Was a Reluctant Caregiver," *Caregivers* (blog), October 22, 2013, http://www.caregivers.com/blog/2013/10/reluctant/.

CHAPTER 14: MONEY TALKS

1. Sharon Burns and Raymond Forgue, *How to Care for Your Parents' Money While Caring for Your Parents* (New York: McGraw-Hill, 2003), 2.
2. "Elder Financial Exploitation," National Adult Protective Services Association, 2015, http://www.napsa-now.org/policy-advocacy/exploitation/.
3. Dave Lindorff, "Going the Extra Mile," *Bank Investment Consultant* 22, no. 8 (October 2014), 23–25.
4. "Elder Financial Exploitation," National Adult Protective Services Association.
5. "Interagency Guidance on Privacy Laws and Reporting Financial Abuse of Older Adults," White Paper, Board of Governors of the Federal Reserve System, 2, http://www.federalreserve.gov/newsevents/press/bcreg/bcreg 20130924a2.pdf.
6. "What Is Financial Exploitation?" National Adult Protective Services Association, 2015, http://www.napsa-now.org/get-informed/what-is-financial-exploitation/.
7. "Elder Financial Exploitation," National Adult Protective Services Association.
8. Dave Ramsey, "How to Talk to Your Parents About Money," *Dave Ramsey* (blog), June 21, 2011, https://www.daveramsey.com/blog/talk-to-your-parents -about-money.
9. Burns and Forgue, *How to Care for Your Parents' Money*, 227.
10. Rick Warren, "Trust Your Finances to God's Provision," *Daily Hope with Rick Warren* (blog), May 21, 2014, http://rickwarren.org/devotional/english/trust -your-finances-to-god's-provision.

CHAPTER 15: GIVE ME A BREAK

1. Denise E. Flori, "Caregiving for the Elderly," American Association for Marriage and Family Therapy, https://www.aamft.org/iMIS15/AAMFT/Content /consumer_updates/caregiving_for_the_elderly.aspx.
2. "Women and Caregiving: Facts and Figures," Family Caregiver Alliance, https:// www.caregiver.org/women-and-caregiving-facts-and-figures.
3. Ibid.
4. Ibid.
5. Gregory L. Jantz, "Brain Differences Between Genders," *Psychology Today*, February 27, 2014, https://www.psychologytoday.com/blog/hope-relationships /201402/brain-differences-between-genders.
6. Ibid.
7. Ibid.
8. "Taking Care of YOU: Self-Care for Family Caregivers," Family Caregiver Alliance, https://caregiver.org/taking-care-you-self-care-family-caregivers.
9. Rosenberger, *Hope for the Caregiver*, 153.
10. Holstege and Riekse, *Caring for Aging Loved Ones*, 81.
11. Celia Watson Seupel, "Broken, Briefly," *The New Old Age* (blog), *New York Times*, December 9, 2011, http://newoldage.blogs.nytimes.com/2011/12/09 /broken-briefly/#more-10861.
12. Ibid.

CHAPTER 16: A DIFFERENT STATE OF MIND

1. Mayo Clinic staff, "Dementia," Patient Care and Health Info, Mayo Clinic, http://www.mayoclinic.org/diseases-conditions/dementia/basics/definition /con-20034399.
2. Sarah Stevenson, "Dementia Care Dos & Don'ts: Dealing with Dementia Behavior Problems," *Senior Living Blog*, January 14, 2016, http://www .aplaceformom.com/blog/2013-02-08-dealing-with-dementia-behavior/.
3. Mayo Clinic staff, "Alzheimer's Care: Simple Tips for Daily Tasks," Mayo Clinic, http://www.mayoclinic.org/healthy-lifestyle/caregivers/in-depth/alzheimers -caregiver/art-20047577.

CHAPTER 18: MARRIAGE AND CAREGIVING

1. Katie Hafner, *Mother Daughter Me* (New York: Random House, Inc., 2013), 185.
2. "80 Percent of Caregivers Report Strain on Their Marriages," Caring.Inc., press release, February 5, 2009, https://www.caring.com/about/news-room/press -release-caregiver-marital-stress.
3. Connie Matthiessen, "Marriage and Relationships: How Caregiving Couples Can Make It Work," Caring.com, https://www.caring.com/articles/caregiving -couples-marriage.

4. Candace Rotolo, "Keeping Relationships Strong While Caregiving: A True Story," AgingCare, https://www.agingcare.com/Articles/caregiving-while -keeping-relationships-intact-148186.htm.
5. "Do Not Obey Your Parents—Boundaries with Mom and Dad," *Boundaries Books* (blog), November 17, 2014, http://www.boundariesbooks.com/boundaries /do-not-obey-parents/.

CHAPTER 19: END-OF-LIFE DECISIONS
1. "Profile of Older Americans: 2012," Administration on Aging, U.S. Department of Health and Human Services, p. 15.
2. Ibid.
3. Brummett, *Take My Hand Again*, 43.
4. Elinor Ginzler, "Which Type of Housing Is Best for You?" AARP, July 2009, http://www.aarp.org/home-garden/housing/info-08-2009/ginzler_housing _choices.html.
5. Ibid.
6. Brandon Bailey, "High-Tech Sensors Help Kids Keep Eye on Aging Parents," Yahoo! Finance, May 5, 2015, finance.yahoo.com/news/high-tech-sensors-help -kids-134415494.html.
7. Jennifer Jolly, "Tech Now: Best New Tech to Help Aging Parents," *USA Today*, May 11, 2014, http://usatoday.com/story/tech/columnist/2014/05/11/tech -gadgets-for-the-elderly/8804955.
8. "Funeral Fights: Breaking Up Families?" Remnant Report, http://remnantreport .com/cgi-bin/imcart/read.cgi?article_id=215&sub=33.
9. Lawrence Solorio, in e-mail to author, December 31, 2015.

FINAL THOUGHTS
1. Holstege and Riekse, *Caring for Aging Loved Ones*, 39.

SUGGESTED RESOURCES

WEBSITES

AARP, AARP.org (caregiving resource center, care provider locator, long-term care calculator)

Administration on Aging, part of the U.S. Department of Health and Human Services, aoa.gov, (800) 677-1116. The eldercare site (eldercare.gov/eldercare.net /index) can help you locate adult day programs, financial and legal assistance, housing options, in-home services, and more.

Alzheimer's Association, Alz.org

Area Agencies on Aging, n4a.org

Christian Caregiver, christiancaregiversupport.com (daily devotions, smartphone app for prescription reminders, book reviews, and a wealth of information for caregivers)

DaveRamsey.com (financial resources, including eldercare)

Family Caregiver Alliance, caregiver.org (individual state listings of programs and services in the Family Care Navigator, as well as other information)

Focus on the Family, focusonthefamily.com (counseling and prayer for life issues such as caregiving)

Home Instead Senior Care, caregiverstress.com (information on end-of-life discussions with loved ones, home care, self-care)

Medicare, medicare.gov (information on home health services, identity theft, as well as medical providers and coverage)

BOOKS

Shelly Beach, *Ambushed by Grace*, Grand Rapids, MI: Discovery House Publishers, 2008.

Nancy Parker Brummett, *Take My Hand Again: A Faith-Based Guide For Helping Aging Parents*, Grand Rapids, MI: Kregel Publications, 2015.

Sharon Burns and Raymond Forgue, *How to Care for Your Parents' Money While Caring for Your Parents*, New York: McGraw-Hill, 2003.

Barbara Deane, *Caring for Your Aging Parents*, Colorado Springs, CO: NavPress, 1989.

Henry Holstege and Robert Riekse, eds., *Complete Guide to Caring for Aging Loved Ones*, Carol Stream, IL: Tyndale House/Focus on the Family, 2002.

Peter Rosenberger, *Hope for the Caregiver*, Brentwood, TN: Worthy Inspired Publishing, 2014.